Praise for
I Want More!

"*I Want More!* weighs the limited experience of the average believer against the dynamic promise of the Holy Spirit's work and power in his or her life. Robert Jeffress reminds us that Spirit-charged living is not the result of an occasional high-voltage worship experience, but rather a daily reliance on the 'Generator'—the Holy Spirit—working on behalf of regenerated men and women. If you want more, this is a book that answers the cry of your heart."

—JACK GRAHAM, pastor of Prestonwood Baptist Church, Plano, Texas

"People go to church because their hearts are hungry, but too often they leave without the spiritual nourishment they need. Why this happens and what to do about it is often discussed, but rarely with the biblical expertise and caring concern Dr. Robert Jeffress brings to the discussion. The reader of *I Want More!* steps into a chapel of warm reverence where the Father's invitation to come to Him is explained not in theological jargon, but with an assuring explanation. The life-changing work of the Holy Spirit is neither hyped nor hidden, simply made available to those who seek His presence."

—HOWARD G. HENDRICKS, Distinguished Professor and chairman, Center for Christian Leadership, Dallas Theological Seminary

"Why are Christians often underwhelmed by the Christian life and overwhelmed by the world? The most fundamental reason is the stunted discipleship and spiritual immaturity so common in the church today. In *I Want More!* Dr. Robert Jeffress provides biblical counsel and real-life application for the Christian life, focusing on the work of the Holy Spirit in the life of the believer. *I Want More!* will bring encouragement and instruction to every believer."

—R. ALBERT MOHLER, JR., president of Southern Baptist
Theological Seminary, Louisville, Kentucky

"Dr. Robert Jeffress adroitly addresses a subject that has been too readily abandoned by evangelical Bible-believing Christians in a reaction against the clear excesses of some. With a knack for making biblical truth easily acceptable to the person in the pew, Robert Jeffress has 'scratched where it itches' in this book."

—PAIGE PATTERSON, Southeastern Baptist Theological Seminary,
Wake Forest, North Carolina

I WANT MORE!

I WANT MORE!

YOU CAN EXPERIENCE

More Joy in Worship

More Power in Prayer

More Success over Struggles

ROBERT JEFFRESS

WATERBROOK
PRESS

I WANT MORE!
PUBLISHED BY WATERBROOK PRESS
2375 Telstar Drive, Suite 160
Colorado Springs, CO 80920
A division of Random House, Inc.

Italics in Scripture quotations reflect the author's added emphasis.

Names in some anecdotes have been changed to protect the identities of the persons involved.

ISBN 1-57856-519-7

Published in association with Yates & Yates, LLP, Literary Agent, Orange, California.

Library of Congress Cataloging-in-Publication Data
Jeffress, Robert, 1955–
   I want more! : You can experience more joy in worship, more power in prayer, more success over struggles / Robert Jeffress.—1st ed.
      p. cm.
   ISBN 1-57856-519-7
   1. Holy Spirit. 2. Christian life. I. Title.
BT121.3 .J44 2003
234' .13—dc21

                                                                        2002151803

Printed in the United States of America
2003—First Edition

10 9 8 7 6 5 4 3 2 1

To Dr. and Mrs. Landrum Leavell—

For more than fifty years of faithfully breaking
the Word of Life to satisfy the hunger of those who "want more."
Thank you for being encouragers and faithful friends
to your pastor and his family.

CONTENTS

One

A Holy Hunger

You Are Not Alone in Your Desire for More

"There's a spot on your mammogram that looks suspicious. To play it safe, I think we should do a biopsy."

In an odd way for Sandra Elliot, her doctor's words were both jolting and yet eerily expected. Sandra had assumed that her yearly checkup would end the same way it had for the last ten years: with a clear report and the perfunctory warning from the physician to keep a close watch on her health. However, the family history of both a mother and an aunt who had died of breast cancer shortly after their sixtieth birthdays haunted Sandra and led her to believe that one day she would meet the same fate.

But if such calamity were to strike, it was supposed to happen much later, *after* her children were grown, *after* she and her husband had enjoyed some time in an empty nest, and *after* she had a chance to rekindle her relationship with God—a relationship that had been relegated to the back burner as Sandra tried to fulfill the endless responsibilities of marriage and motherhood. But in the back of her mind was the confidence that one day she and God would resume their intimate relationship that had begun twenty-five years earlier at a youth camp, where Sandra had become a Christian.

She could still remember her insatiable spiritual hunger after that experience. She had kept a spiritual journal filled with miraculous answers to prayer. She confronted both friends and family members about their relationship with God with a boldness that was uncharacteristic of most fifteen-year-old girls. She read the Bible voraciously, hiding under the covers with a flashlight to read after her parents had demanded "Lights out."

What a difference twenty-five years can make. Now Sandra had difficulty finding the time—or the desire—to follow her pastor's suggestion of reading one chapter of Proverbs each day. When a friend in Junior League confided that she was severely depressed, Sandra knew this was a great opportunity to share her faith. But fearful of her friend's reaction, she simply recommended that her friend see a therapist. And as far as miraculous answers to prayer go, Sandra had not seen one of those in a long time. In fact, Sandra had pretty much given up on praying after God ignored her request for her mom's healing. Sandra used "the sovereignty of God" as a convenient excuse for her unanswered prayers. But in more contemplative moments, Sandra wondered if there even *was* a God.

Now that she was facing the greatest potential crisis of her forty years, two questions raced through Sandra's mind.

The first was, *Why is God allowing this to happen to me?*

Was this crisis a test from God, designed to strengthen her faith? Sandra recalled a sermon her pastor had recently preached on testing in which he reminded the congregation that God only tests the faithful, not the faithless. Using the examples of Abraham and Job, the pastor said, "Tests are God's vote of confidence in us."

But Sandra doubted that God had very much confidence in her. A much more likely answer to the "Why" question was that God (if He did exist) had sent this problem as a way of disciplining her for twenty-five years of spiritual negligence. He had to get her attention somehow, and surely there could be no more effective way than this.

Which led to Sandra's second question: *What does God want me to do?*

Her best friend from high school, Beth, was also a Christian. But Beth's spiritual experience as a young adult had led her down a different path. Sandra had always considered some of Beth's beliefs about healing, miracles, and "speaking in tongues" a little strange, but certainly tolerable. When Sandra's mother was sick, Beth had strongly encouraged her friend to bring her mother to Beth's church for a special service of prayer and anointing with oil for the sick. Sandra could not bring herself to even ask her mother to attend. But after her mom died, Sandra did attend services with Beth a few times. Although the worship style was so different from that of her church (no one would ever dance in the aisles at Community Bible Church), Sandra felt a spiritual stirring that had been dormant since her high-school days.

Now, in light of her current crisis, Sandra wondered if it was time to take a new look at her relationship with God. Could it be that what she had been taught about faith, prayer, miracles, and the Holy Spirit was wrong? Was her mother's death really the result of God's sovereignty or Sandra's lack of faith? Was this whole crisis a spiritual wake-up call for a new kind of relationship with God, emphasizing the heart over the head—a relationship to be experienced rather than studied? As Sandra watched the vitality of her friend's relationship with God and remembered the sensations she experienced years ago, she became convinced that there is something more. And the report from her doctor made her all the more desperate to discover what that "something more" is.

≋

Jim Sanders could not believe the images that were flickering from his computer. Such pictures would have caused his father to turn away in disgust—no small feat given the fact that Jim's dad had introduced him to the world of pornography when he was a teenager (not directly, of course, but through the stacks of *Playboy* magazines hidden in his father's "special" cabinet, which was off-limits to everyone in the family). But the Internet sites Jim frequented were definitely not his father's pornography. The pictures of men, women, and children involved in indescribable acts reached out from the computer screen like the tentacles of an octopus and pulled Jim into a world from which he had spent years trying to escape.

As a teenager, Jim had assuaged his guilt with periodic trips to the altar at his church to "rededicate" his life to Christ. But his renewed commitments usually lasted until the next issue of *Playboy* found its way into Dad's cabinet. Although Jim was discouraged over his lack of consistent victory over pornography—and the resulting sins—he felt certain that once he was married and had a legitimate outlet for his sexual urges, his habits (and accompanying guilt) would be things of the past.

But fifteen years of marriage and two affairs (one sexual, the other emotional) had only intensified Jim's sexual appetite. After a prayer breakfast at his church one Tuesday morning, the men's leader had invited the participants to find someone they knew in the room to pray with. Jim immediately gravitated toward Ron, a long-time friend. "Jim, what can I pray for you about?" Ron asked. Normally, Jim would have offered several "safe" topics: job, family, opportunities to share God's love at work. But that morning Jim was so overwhelmed with guilt over last night's viewing session—and his wife's sudden discovery of it—that he poured out his heart to Ron about his addiction to pornography.

"Jim, I'm going to pray for you," Ron promised, "but I also want you to come with me to a men's rally at Crowley Stadium this Saturday."

Jim agreed. The following Saturday he, Ron, and fifteen thousand other men listened as a lineup of leading Christian speakers addressed various topics. But it was the final speaker who made Jim realize why God had brought him to the stadium that day. The speaker closed his message with these words:

> There are some of you today who are battling with the sin of pornography. You have tried and tried to win this battle, but you live in constant defeat. Make no mistake about it. This is a spiritual battle, and the only way you can win a spiritual battle is by spiritual power. Right now I am inviting those who are fighting this battle to come to the altar so that you can experience spiritual deliverance from the stranglehold of the Evil One.

Without thinking twice, Jim moved out of his seat toward the platform. As the speaker prayed for Jim and what must have been a thousand other men, tears of relief streamed down Jim's face. He knew that his life would never be the same again. The Holy Spirit had finally delivered him from his sexual demons.

For the next month Jim had absolutely no desire to even go near a computer. The time previously dedicated to chat rooms was replaced with time reading the Bible. He and his wife, Sherri, were experiencing a renewed physical intimacy that had long been absent from their marriage. But in one evening everything changed. Jim was innocently reading the online edition of the *Washington Post* one night when a pop-up advertisement appeared on his screen for a new pornographic site.

Without a moment's hesitancy, Jim clicked the *Accept* button and found himself back in the world from which he thought he had been permanently delivered. When he finally shut down his computer that evening, Jim sat in the darkness and wondered, *Was my experience last month at the stadium real? If it is true that "greater is He who is in me than He who is in the world," why can't "He" give me any victory over this sin? What good is the Holy Spirit if He can't at least put up a little struggle in my battle against pornography?*

~

As he maneuvered his car out of the parking lot and headed home, Roger Simpkins thought to himself, *I'm not sure how many more of these deacons' meetings I can attend.* In his twenty-five years of pastoring churches, Roger had experienced his share of cantankerous meetings, but tonight's had not been one of them. In fact, the only item on the agenda had been the approval of the budget for the coming year. The questions had been predictable, polite, but nevertheless a little painful. "Why are you proposing an increase in the budget if we are not meeting this year's requirements? Is it wise to be raising the budget when the reports show that the church is not growing? Have you noticed that we seem to be losing more members than normal to other churches?"

The last question stung most of all. Yes, the pastor *had* noticed the steady stream of people heading for the exits. At first it was easy to label the departees as "malcontents" and remind people that "sometimes a church has to be pruned before it can grow." But there sure seemed to be a lot of pruning going on lately, and little resulting growth.

As the meeting was breaking up that evening, one of the laymen pulled Roger off to the side and said, "I have just finished reading a book I want to give you. I think it has the answer for what our church needs." Roger thanked the deacon and accepted the book, thinking, *Just what I need, one more thing to read.* Later that evening, after picking at the dinner his wife had kept warm for him and surfing the television channels in a vain attempt to find something interesting, Roger decided to glance at the book.

In the opening chapter, the author talked about the hunger most churches have for a real manifestation of the power and presence of God. He then related an incident that had transformed his ministry forever. While preaching at a friend's church, the power of God had suddenly appeared in the sanctuary and split the Plexiglas pulpit in two! People immediately poured down the aisle to repent of their sins, and thus began weeks of unending revival that revolutionized the church and the city.

Roger was naturally skeptical. A Plexiglas pulpit splitting in two? Come on! The only way a Plexiglas pulpit would split in two at the Pleasant Valley Baptist Church would be if the deacons attacked it with a hammer—which they would most certainly do if such an eyesore were ever installed in their very traditional church.

But as Roger read on, he became convinced that the author was on to something. Yes, most churches were in a state of spiritual starvation. No, the answer was not another program or sermon series. What Roger's church needed was a supernatural visitation by the Holy Spirit.

The following Sunday morning the pastor set aside his series on the tabernacle (for which most of the congregants were grateful) and said he was going to "speak from my heart." For the next thirty minutes he poured out his frustrations about the spiritual stagnation of the congregation and the need for true revival.

> The only way we are ever going to experience the supernatural power and presence of God is by making prayer a priority in our church. Charles Spurgeon once said, "The best style of prayer is that which cannot be called anything else but a cry." God invites us individually and corporately to cry out to him. "Call to me and I will answer you and tell you great and unsearchable things you do not know."[1]

Pastor Simpkins then closed his message with this invitation:

If, like me, you desire the supernatural power and presence
of God in your life and in the life of this church, I want to
invite you to a special prayer service here in the sanctuary
at seven o'clock Tuesday night. There will be no sermon,
no music, but just a time of prayer. Whether two or two
hundred show up, I am going to be here every Tuesday
night crying out to God. And I invite whoever will to
join me.

Two nights later Roger was both surprised and gratified at the
turnout. Over one hundred members came to the prayer meeting.
After expressing his appreciation for the size of the group, Roger
invited everyone to the altar to kneel for prayer. Although there
were a few moments of awkward silence, the hour was pretty well
filled with heartfelt prayers of petitions for healing, revival, and reconciliation. Finally, after an uncomfortably long period of silence,
the pastor decided the crowd was spiritually spent and closed with
a prayer himself.

Several deacons and members huddled around Roger as the
crowd dispersed.

"Pastor, this is the most meaningful prayer time I've ever been
a part of."

"This is exactly what our church needs."

"This is a new beginning for our church!"

The following Tuesday night about seventy-five people showed
up for the prayer service. Although Roger knew the momentum
would be hard to maintain, this was still a respectable crowd. After
the session fewer people stayed around to talk with the pastor.
Everyone seemed eager to get home. Over the next two months the

prayer warriors dwindled down to the faithful fifteen. Roger tried to encourage them with little spiritual bromides such as, "Jesus said, 'Where two or three are gathered together I am with them,'" and "It took only twelve men to turn the world upside down for Christ."

But deep down—and not really that deep—Roger was disappointed. What was wrong with his church? What was wrong with him? Why didn't this commitment to prayer bring about the spiritual transformation that the book had promised? Is this so-called spiritual hunger that Christians are supposed to have real or something book publishers and professional church leaders have manufactured to make a buck? If this hunger is real, then why do so few Christians have a desire to satisfy it?

SPIRITUALLY SHORTCHANGED?

Sandra Elliot, Jim Sanders, and Roger Simpkins share something in common: They believe that their Christian faith has promised more than it has actually delivered. They all feel that they have been spiritually shortchanged. The miraculous healings, supernatural power, and dynamic worship that other Christians and congregations are experiencing have eclipsed them. And they wonder why.

I don't believe that Sandra, Jim, and Roger are atypical. In my experience as a pastor, I have discovered that in their most honest moments the majority of Christians do not believe that their relationship with God has made any significant difference in their day-to-day lives. Just like non-Christians, they experience conflict in their marriages, rebellion in their children, financial needs in their bank accounts, struggles in their moral lives, and disease in their bodies. Secretly, they hope that Jesus is better at delivering the eternal life He promised for the next life than the abundant life He promised for this one.

Chuck Swindoll describes the spiritual vacuum many Christians feel:

> The inescapable fact is this: Most (yes, most) Christians you and I know have very little dynamic [Chuck's word for "power"] or joy in their lives. Just ask them. They long for depth, for passion, for a satisfying peace and stability instead of a superficial relationship with God made up of words without feelings and struggles without healings. Surely there is more to the life of faith than church meetings, Bible study, religious jargon, and periodic prayers. Surely the awesome Spirit of God wishes to do more within us than what is presently going on![2]

IS SOMETHING MISSING?

Let's turn the spotlight on you for a moment. I want you to take a few thoughtful seconds to honestly answer the following four questions about yourself. No need to share your answers with anyone. This is just between you and God.

1. Is there a measurable difference between your relationship with God when you were a new believer and now? Is that relationship more intimate or more distant?
2. Other than how you spend your time on Sunday mornings, what is the *real* difference between your life and that of non-Christians you know?
3. Can you cite several occurrences in your life (answers to prayer, physical healings, financial needs met, or relationships reconciled) that could *only* be explained by the supernatural working of God?

4. Do you know other Christians who seem to be experiencing more joy and power in their relationship with God than you are?

I don't know you, and you don't know much about me yet, but I imagine the reason you are reading this book is that at least one of the following is true about you:

- The level of *excitement* (or *joy* or *commitment*—you fill in the blank) in your Christian life has diminished significantly since you first became a Christian.
- The difference between you and the most morally upright non-Christian you know is limited to your beliefs.
- You have difficulty identifying at least three miracles in your life.
- You find yourself struggling repeatedly with the same sins.
- Sunday worship has become more of an endurance contest than an encounter with God.
- You find it difficult to consistently read the Bible.
- When you pray about a difficult situation, deep down you really don't expect God to do anything.
- You sense that there is something missing in your relationship with God.

If any or all of the above statements are true about you, don't despair. Your ability even to recognize that there may be something missing in your relationship with God is evidence that He is working in your life. You're becoming more aware of a "holy hunger" within you that God wants to satisfy. You are beginning to form the crucial question that is the foundation of this book: "What must I do to experience more of God's supernatural power in my life?"

But now that you have been honest about your spiritual shortcomings, allow me to lay *my* cards on the table as well. Each of the above statements has been (and some still are) true of my life—and of the lives of the majority of people to whom I minister.

INCREASED "DISCONNECT" BETWEEN BELIEF AND BEHAVIOR

I recently asked a psychiatrist friend of mine, "What difference do you see in the lives of the Christians and non-Christians you treat?"

Her answer? "Absolutely none."

Think about what an astounding observation that is! From her vantage point, Christians are just as prone to marital conflict, sexual immorality, drug addiction, and suicide as non-Christians. Admittedly, this is one person's observation, but a growing number of studies seem to indicate that the lifestyle differences between people of the Christian faith, of some other faith, or of no faith are negligible. Christians are living in the same kind of spiritual bondage as non-Christians. Something is definitely wrong with this picture! Especially when you try to reconcile the experience of most Christians with the apostle Paul's words:

> Our old self was crucified with Him, in order that our
> body of sin might be done away with, so that we would no
> longer be slaves to sin; for he who has died is freed from
> sin. (Romans 6:6-7)

INCREASED DISBELIEF IN GOD'S SUPERNATURAL POWER

Recently a distressed member of our congregation called me with a desperate need. Her husband's cancerous tumor was growing in spite of the chemotherapy he had endured for the past three months.

"Pastor, would you please pray for him?"

I did pray, but, I'm ashamed to admit, more out of duty than conviction. I really didn't expect God to do anything. Why not? Part of my reluctance to pray came from experience. I have watched dozens upon dozens of Christians go through the same cycle: discovery of a disease, treatment for the disease, and eventually, death from the disease. Prayers offered between discovery and treatment or treatment and death rarely, if ever, change the eventual outcome.

But my (and perhaps your) reluctance to pray for God's supernatural intervention in our lives also stems from a basic theological assumption that goes something like this: "God does not perform miracles today in the same way that He did in biblical times. In fact, as you look through the Bible, you will discover that there are only three periods in which God performed miracles: the days of Moses and Joshua, the time of Elijah and Elisha, and the time of Christ and the apostles. Now that we have the Bible, there is no longer any need for miracles."

Have you ever heard that theory expressed? The technical name for this belief is *cessation*—that is, the miraculous gifts and events recorded in the Bible have "ceased." I was heavily influenced in my younger years by gifted and well-meaning Bible teachers who came to the conclusion that God no longer performs miracles (though they would never say it quite that strongly). Today I do not believe that either Scripture or experience supports that view. The Bible is filled with examples from Genesis to Revelation of God supernaturally intervening in the lives of His people. If God is no longer in the business of miracles, then why did James offer this advice to those who are ill?

> Is anyone among you sick? Then he must call for the elders of the church and they are to pray over him, anointing him with oil in the name of the Lord; and the prayer offered in faith will restore the one who is sick, and the Lord will raise him up, and if he has committed sins, they will be forgiven him. (James 5:14-15)

Increased Discontent with the Status Quo

Ronald Reagan once defined *status quo* as "Latin for 'the mess we're in.'" My observation is that a growing number of Christians are disillusioned and discontent with their spiritual condition. They are tired of going through the motions. They are weary of giving lip service to truths that have made little difference in their lives. As a result, they are gravitating toward churches that emphasize experience over exposition, heart over head. They long for something more.

I understand that desire. My father was led to Christ shortly after the Second World War by an Assembly of God chaplain. After my dad's discharge from the service, he moved to a large city in Texas. When he asked his spiritual mentor for a suggestion about where to attend church, the chaplain directed him to a Baptist church known for its sound doctrinal teaching. My father followed his advice and joined that congregation. He later led my mom to Christ and she, too, became a part of that wonderful congregation in which I was later reared.

But my dad was never completely content in that church. He felt that something was missing. So after attending the Baptist church on Sunday mornings, he would take us to an Assembly of God church on Sunday evenings. That's where I was dedicated to the Lord at two years of age. Some of my earliest memories as a child are of those evening services that were noticeably more lively than my Sunday morning worship experiences.

My father spent the rest of his life spiritually conflicted. Although he was conservative in his theology and strongly encouraged me to attend Dallas Theological Seminary, he could never completely discount speaking in tongues, a second work of the Holy Spirit, miraculous healings, and other phenomena associated with the charismatic movement. Until the day he died of pancreatic cancer, my father was convinced that there was "something more" to the Christian faith than what he had experienced personally.

As I look back on the conversations we had while I was a theology student and beginning pastor, I recall our good-natured but heated arguments. With great conviction, I argued that the miraculous events of the Bible had ceased, that there were no more experiences with the Holy Spirit after salvation, that we could not expect complete deliverance from sin while we still carried around a sin nature, and that charismatic churches were rooted in emotionalism rather than spiritual reality.

However, I am now willing to admit that I was wrong and my father was right. (I can only imagine the smiling "I told you so" that awaits me when I join him in heaven.) Indeed, there *is* something more to a relationship with God than merely trusting in Jesus for our salvation while trying to muddle through this life the best we can until we die.

In the following pages we are going to discover what that "something more" is.

Two

YOU'RE RICHER THAN
YOU THINK!

Check Under the Hood Before You Trade In Your Faith

An old Indian chief living in Oklahoma hit oil one day on his small parcel of land on the reservation. Suddenly he had more money than Jed Clampett and could purchase anything he wanted. There was only one luxury he really desired: a Cadillac. He went to the local car dealership, handed the salesman a wad of thousand-dollar bills, and purchased the largest and most powerful model available.

Every morning the chief would drive around the town square in his red Cadillac. However, his driving left a lot to be desired. Instead of concentrating on the road, the chief would turn to his left and engage friends on the sidewalks in conversation; he would then turn to the right and wave at other friends. Occasionally he would even stand up in the front seat and turn around to greet those behind him.

But no one really felt threatened by the chief's driving habits. Instead, people smiled and waved back at the chief as they observed him in his shiny new red automobile—drawn by the two horses he had hitched to the front of the Cadillac.

Many Christians are like that old Indian chief. They saunter through life without any awareness of the tremendous spiritual horsepower they already possess. Lulled into spiritual complacency, they are content to travel no farther or faster than they are now moving. They have convinced themselves that

- they never can enjoy consistent victory over sin;
- they should not anticipate miraculous answers to their prayers;
- they never should expect God to speak to them; and
- they have made too many compromises to ever experience the power and presence of God in their lives.

However, others are no longer satisfied to keep wandering around the way they have been for the past few years. You may be among them. You want *more*. As you watch other "super-Christians" whiz by you, you wonder if you need to trade in your faith for a shinier and faster model that promises more.

Before you make that decision, you need to consider what you already own. Read your owner's manual (the Bible), and you will discover that underneath your spiritual "hood" is a powerful engine that has all the spiritual horsepower you need in life. His name is the Holy Spirit, and He is the focus of our attention in this chapter.

WHO IS THE HOLY SPIRIT?

This book is an attempt to answer the question, "How can I experience more of God's power in my life?" The short answer is, "By understanding and cooperating with the Holy Spirit's work in your life." However, such an answer is obviously not enough to fill an entire book, so some further explanation is warranted. If the Holy Spirit is the answer to our deepest spiritual longing, then we need to understand who the Holy Spirit is, as well as His role in the life of the believer. While this chapter is not intended to be a doctrinal treatise on the Holy Spirit, there are two aspects of His being that I want to be sure you are aware of.

THE HOLY SPIRIT IS GOD

I have a pastor friend who says that while growing up he never thought of the godhead as a trinity (three Persons in one), but as a dynamic duo—God the Father and Jesus Christ the Son. But the Bible clearly teaches that the Holy Spirit is equal to God…because He *is* God.

Genesis 1:2 tells us that the Holy Spirit was involved in the creation of the world: "The Spirit of God was moving over the surface of the waters."

In Matthew 28:19, Jesus commands us to baptize people in the name of "the Father and the Son and the Holy Spirit."

The apostle Paul equated the Holy Spirit with God when he wrote, "The grace of the Lord Jesus Christ, and the love of God, and the fellowship of the Holy Spirit, be with you all" (2 Corinthians 13:14).

The apostle Peter said that lying to the Holy Spirit was tantamount to lying to God. When Peter rebuked Ananias he asked, "Why has Satan filled your heart to lie to the Holy Spirit…? You have not lied to men but to God" (Acts 5:3-4).

I hear a collective "So what?" coming from some of my readers, so I need you to stay with me for a few more pages as we uncover what this truth means in our everyday lives. But until we get there, think about this reality for a moment: To say that the Holy Spirit lives in you is to say that *God* lives in you. If you have trusted Jesus Christ as your Savior and Lord, then the same power of God that flung billions of galaxies into existence with just a few words, that fed five thousand people with five loaves and two fishes, and that raised Jesus Christ from the dead is at work in *your* life—right now—in some very specific ways! Close your eyes and contemplate the significance of this truth:

The power of God resides in me.

If you are a Christian, the power of God resides in you because *God Himself* lives within you. This is the bottom line of Christianity. As A. W. Tozer exclaimed,

> Deity indwelling men! That, I say, is Christianity, and no man has experienced rightly the power of Christian belief until he has known this for himself as a living reality. Everything else is preliminary to this.[1]

THE HOLY SPIRIT IS ALSO A PERSON

Not only is the Holy Spirit God, but He is a Person. This is why the New Testament refers to the Holy Spirit as "He," not as "it."

What do I mean by "Person"? Well, what is it that distinguishes you from the book you are holding? You have *thoughts*...but this book never thinks about anything. You also have a *will;* you decided to open this book, and at some point you will choose to put this book down (hopefully not before the end of this chapter). But the book you're reading has no will; it never says, "As soon as this clown closes me, I think I'll have lunch." You also have *emotions;* you laugh, cry, get excited, and sometimes feel depressed. But this book never smiled or shed a single tear. Intellect, will, and emotion distinguish a person from an object.

The Holy Spirit is a Person because He possesses *intellect.* For example, He is able to understand what none of us can ever hope to comprehend: the thoughts of God. "For who among men knows the thoughts of a man except the spirit of the man which is in him? Even so the thoughts of God no one knows except the Spirit of God" (1 Corinthians 2:11).

The Holy Spirit also has a *will.* He makes decisions. For example, He determines which spiritual gifts He will give to various people. "But one and the same Spirit works all these things, distributing to each one individually just as He wills" (1 Corinthians 12:11).

Finally, the Holy Spirit experiences *emotions,* just as we all do. For example, Romans 15:30 refers to "the love of the Spirit." Objects don't love; only people love. The Bible also warns us not to "grieve the Holy Spirit" (Ephesians 4:30). You can throw this book on the floor and stomp on it, but you will never cause it to feel any pain. But God says it is possible for our behavior to bring deep sadness to the Holy Spirit.

How and When Does the Holy Spirit Come into Our Lives?

Obviously, the answer to this question has profound implications. If I am a Christian, do I need to beg the Holy Spirit to come into my life? Are there some exercises I need to perform to persuade Him to empower me? If He is already present within me, why am I not experiencing His power the way other people do? Is there some spiritual "switch" I need to turn on to activate His energy?

Philip Yancey offers some insightful words about Christians who are constantly searching for the Holy Spirit:

> To search for the Spirit is like hunting for your eyeglasses while wearing them. In John V. Taylor's words, "We can never be directly aware of the Spirit, since in any experience of meeting and recognition he is always the go-between

who creates awareness." The Spirit is what we perceive with rather than what we perceive, the one who opens our eyes to underlying spirit-ual realities.[2]

Now I realize some readers do not believe that every Christian permanently possesses the Holy Spirit. You can point to some New Testament passages to indicate that the coming of the Holy Spirit is subsequent to salvation. You can cite countless examples of believers who testify to an additional experience with the Holy Spirit after salvation. And you ask a very reasonable question: If the Holy Spirit lives in every Christian, why isn't every Christian experiencing more

- joy in his worship?
- supernatural answers to her prayers?
- consistent victory over sin?
- overflowing love in his heart?

You have a point! In fact, the above questions should cause *all* of us to seriously reexamine what we believe about the working of the Holy Spirit in our lives. After seriously reconsidering my own beliefs about the Holy Spirit, I have come to this conclusion, which I would like you to consider with me in this and the next section:

> While every Christian is *indwelt* by the Holy Spirit,
> not every Christian is *empowered* by the Holy Spirit.

As I will demonstrate in this chapter, the Scriptures teach quite clearly (with a few exceptions we shall examine) that the moment a person trusts in Christ as Savior, the Holy Spirit sets up permanent residence in his or her life. But there is a vast difference between experiencing the *indwelling* of the Holy Spirit and experiencing the *power* of the Holy Spirit, as we will see in the next chapter.

The Baptism with the Spirit

Let's return to our car illustration for a moment. Suppose our Indian chief friend had attached two horses to his new Cadillac because it actually lacked any mechanical "horsepower." That is, when the chief went into the dealership and inquired about the cost of the automobile, the salesman replied, "It depends."

"Depends on what?" the chief asked.

"On whether you want an engine with your car. Without an engine, the car costs twenty thousand dollars; with an engine it'll be thirty thousand dollars."

While every car has "optional" equipment available for purchase, who would ever consider an engine optional? In the same way, the Holy Spirit is not an optional benefit to be added after one becomes a Christian. He is part of the basic package. No, change that—He *is* the basic passage! That truth is what Tozer had in mind when he wrote about "deity indwelling man" as the essence of Christianity.

The biblical phrase used to describe the Holy Spirit's act of entering our lives is *baptism with the Spirit,* and it is explained by Paul in 1 Corinthians 12:13: "For by one Spirit we were all baptized into one body, whether Jews or Greeks, whether slaves or free, and we were all made to drink of one Spirit."

Remember that Paul was writing to the church at Corinth—a church severely divided over such trivial issues as their favorite pastor, spiritual gifts, the role of women in the church, and contemporary versus traditional worship. (Okay, I made that last one up, but I wouldn't be surprised if they argued over that, too.) In 1 Corinthians 12, Paul explained that God intends for there to be both diversity and unity in the church. God never meant for Christians to look alike, believe exactly alike, or like the same kind of music. And yet, Jesus prayed that "they may be one even as We are" (John 17:11).

How can diversity and unity coexist in the same organization? Just look in the mirror, Paul tells us! You are not one giant eyeball or one humongous nostril. No, your body consists of many different parts, and yet you are one person.

> For even as the body is one and yet has many members, and all the members of the body, though they are many, are one body, so also is Christ. (1 Corinthians 12:12)

Just as the human body demonstrates unity in diversity, so does the church, which is the body of Christ. God took people with varying gifts, contrasting personalities, and differing cultural backgrounds and joined them together in one organism. How did He pull that off? Through baptism with the Holy Spirit (see again 1 Corinthians 12:13).

To understand what Paul was teaching about baptism with the Holy Spirit, let's consider four key words in this simple yet profound verse.

"Baptized"

The word *baptized* comes from the Greek word *baptizo* and has one and only one meaning: "immersed." The word was used in Greek literature to describe the process by which a piece of cloth would be dipped into a container of dye in order to change the color of the cloth. If you wanted to change the color of a piece of fabric from red to purple, you would not simply sprinkle a few drops of purple dye onto the red cloth; you would "baptize" it completely in the container of purple dye.

Now when some of my fellow Baptists read the word *baptized,* they get all excited and want to turn down the lights, crank up the organ music, and jump into a pool of water. While water baptism is certainly an important symbol of what happens when a person trusts Christ as Savior, that is not the kind of baptism Paul had in mind here. Baptism with the Spirit is "dry" rather than "wet."

When God baptizes us with the Holy Spirit, He changes our spiritual "color" completely. He transforms us from rebellious, guilty sinners into obedient and righteous disciples by immersing us with His Holy Spirit.

"With"

Many Christians freely speak of the "baptism *of* the Holy Spirit," a phrase never found in the Bible. Instead, the Scriptures always speak of the baptism *with* the Holy Spirit or the baptism *by* (meaning "with") the Holy Spirit. You may be wondering, *So what? What difference does a little preposition make?* A lot! When people refer to "the baptism *of* the Holy Spirit," the implication is that it is the Holy Spirit who does the baptizing. No wonder, then, that many Christians today pray to the Holy Spirit, asking Him to come into their lives. Yet the Bible clearly teaches that Jesus Christ, not the Holy Spirit, is our spiritual baptizer. Jesus baptizes us *with* or *by means of* the Holy Spirit:

> I [John the Baptist] baptized you with water; but He [Jesus] will baptize you with the Holy Spirit. (Mark 1:8)

> I [John the Baptist] did not recognize Him [Jesus], but He who sent me to baptize in water said to me, "He upon whom you see the Spirit descending and remaining upon Him, this is the One who baptizes in the Holy Spirit."
> (John 1:33)

Paul affirmed the same truth in 1 Corinthians 12:13. The word translated *by* means "by means of" or "with." Think about the act of water baptism for a moment. Who does the baptizing?

Does the water ever rise up and say, "I baptize you, John Smith"? No, the pastor (representing Christ) is the baptizer, and the water (representing the Holy Spirit) is what the pastor baptizes *with*. In the same way, Jesus is the One who baptizes us with the spiritual water of the Holy Spirit.

"Were"

The tense of the word *baptized* in 1 Corinthians 12:13 indicates that this is an action that had already occurred in the lives of the Corinthians. They were not waiting to be baptized with the Holy Spirit. They had already been immersed with the Holy Spirit.

But what about all of those passages in the Bible that seem to indicate that the coming of the Holy Spirit into a Christian's life occurs after salvation rather than at the time of salvation? In his excellent book *God in You,* David Jeremiah explains three categories of passages in the Bible dealing with the coming of the Holy Spirit.

1. *Expectancy.* These passages in the Old Testament and the Gospels anticipate the coming of the Holy Spirit. "It will come about after this that I will pour out My Spirit on all mankind" (Joel 2:28). "John answered and said to them all, 'As for me, I baptize you with water; but One is coming who is mightier than I.... He will baptize you with the Holy Spirit and fire" (Luke 3:16).

2. *Experience.* The book of Acts records the actual coming of the Holy Spirit into believers' lives. As Peter recounted what had happened on the Day of Pentecost when the Holy Spirit first came into the lives of believers, he said, "And I remembered the word of the Lord, how He used to say, 'John baptized with water, but you will be baptized with the Holy Spirit'" (Acts 11:16).

3. *Explanation.* Found mainly in the Epistles, these passages explain the benefits of baptism with the Holy Spirit. "Do you not know that all of us who have been baptized into Christ Jesus have been baptized into His death? Therefore we have been buried with Him through baptism into death, so that as Christ was raised from the dead through the glory of the Father, so we too might walk in newness of life" (Romans 6:3-4).

A careful study of these passages reveals that the baptism with the Holy Spirit is not some future event to be anticipated and sought after; instead, it is a spiritual reality that every believer has *already* experienced.

But what about the passages in Acts that picture those who are already saved and are waiting for the coming of the Holy Spirit? Books such as *God in You* that deal exclusively with the doctrine of the Holy Spirit can offer more extensive answers to that question, but allow me to give a brief explanation for each of the three instances in Acts where the baptism with the Holy Spirit appears to happen subsequent to salvation.

Acts 2:1-4. This passage records the coming of the Holy Spirit into the lives of believers—an event that the Old Testament prophets, John the Baptist, and even Jesus Christ anticipated. Jesus clearly taught that the Holy Spirit could not come until Jesus ascended into heaven: "But I tell you the truth, it is to your advantage that I go away; for if I do not go away, the Helper [the Holy Spirit] will not come to you; but if I go, I will send Him to you" (John 16:7).

Just as there was one point in history when Christ was born and another point in history when He was raised from the dead, there was also one unrepeatable moment in time when the Holy Spirit came in fulfillment of the long-anticipated promises. The late Merrill Unger wrote, "Pentecost is as unrepeatable as the creation of the world and of man; as once-for-all as the incarnation and the death, resurrection, and ascension."[3]

Acts 8:14-17. In this passage it is clear that there were believers in Samaria who did not receive the Holy Spirit the moment they believed. Instead, they had to wait for the arrival of the leaders of the Jerusalem church before the Holy Spirit came into their lives. Why the delay? God was demonstrating to these new Samaritan Christians (who hated and were hated by the Jews) that they were under the authority of Peter, John, and the other leaders of the church in Jerusalem.

Acts 19:1-7. The apostle Paul found a group of people who appeared to be Christians in the upper region of Ephesus. Like any good evangelist, Paul wanted to make sure of their conversion. Instead of asking them, "If you were to stand before God, and He were to ask you, 'Why should I let you into heaven?' what would you say?" Paul posed another diagnostic question: "Have you received the Holy Spirit?" Obviously, Paul believed that baptism with the Holy Spirit was the norm for every Christian. When they answered, "We don't know what you're talking about!" Paul probed a little further and discovered they weren't believers in Christ at all, but followers of John the Baptist. After the gospel was explained to them, they believed in Christ and were baptized with the Holy Spirit.

The pattern from the days of Acts 8 through today is clear: Every genuine Christian is baptized with the Holy Spirit at the moment of his or her salvation.[4]

"All"

This little word is filled with significance. Remember to whom Paul was expressing the truth of baptism with the Holy Spirit: the Corinthians! Hardly a group of spiritual giants. They were constantly fighting with one another, getting drunk at the Lord's

Supper, and committing every kind of sexual immorality. Yet Paul affirmed that *even they* had been baptized with the Holy Spirit:

> For by one Spirit we were *all* baptized into one body,
> whether Jews or Greeks, whether slaves or free, and we were
> all made to drink of one Spirit. (1 Corinthians 12:13)

This passage should drive a stake through the erroneous idea that baptism with the Holy Spirit is an experience reserved for some special class of super-Christians. Baptism with the Holy Spirit is not a spiritual "upgrade" for those willing to pay extra for a first-class relationship with God. Instead, it is a reality for every believer.

What Does the Holy Spirit Mean to You?

Now that you have waded with me through some deep doctrinal waters, let's get practical. What does the indwelling of the Holy Spirit mean to me? While there are numerous benefits of baptism with the Holy Spirit, let me mention just three.

The Holy Spirit Gives Us the Ability to Trust in Christ

Is everyone in the world free to trust Jesus Christ as personal Savior? Absolutely! Jesus repeatedly made it clear that anyone who wants to come to Him may do so; He would never turn a sincere seeker away. The only problem is that no one ever chooses to come to Christ of his or her own free will. Ever!

If you have difficulty believing that, perhaps the following illustration will help.

If you place a bale of hay in front of a lion, is the lion free to eat the hay? Yes, he is free to gorge himself with as much hay as he desires, but he never will chose to do so. Why? By nature he is a carnivore, meaning that he eats only meat. So no matter how many opportunities you give a lion, he will never choose hay. To change a lion's appetite, you have to change his nature.[5]

The same is true about us. The Bible says that "by nature" we are "children of wrath" who are "dead in [our] trespasses and sins" (Ephesians 2:1,3). In other words, we are born with absolutely no appetite for God. The "hunger for God" that some unbelievers claim to have may be a desire for a god of their own making, but not for the true God. Paul stated quite bluntly, "There is none who seeks for God" (Romans 3:11). As "children of wrath," we are born with a natural aversion to God.

As if that were not bad enough, Paul went on to assert that we are also incapable of responding to God at all—"dead in...trespasses and sins." As a pastor, my job requires me to spend an inordinate amount of time around dead people. At a recent funeral I was standing at the head of a casket as people passed by to pay their last respects. As I turned to give a pastoral look of compassionate respect to the dearly departed, I spotted the biggest fly I have ever seen sitting on the nose of the corpse! When there was a short gap in the crowd passing by the casket, I discreetly reached over and swatted the fly. Amazingly, Mr. Jones did not blink, flinch, or sneeze. Why? He was dead.

In the same way, Paul said that we are born into this world spiritually dead, unable to respond to the gospel message no matter how forcefully or frequently someone shares the truth with us. So how does anyone ever become a Christian? Paul explained:

> But God, being rich in mercy, because of His great love
> with which He loved us, even when we were dead in
> our transgressions, *made us alive* together with Christ.
> (Ephesians 2:4-5)

God is the One who gives us the ability to trust in Christ as our Savior. He does this by making us who were spiritually dead "alive in the spirit" (1 Peter 3:18). It is by the Holy Spirit's work that we are made aware of our sin, that we understand the significance of Jesus' death on the cross for our sins, and that we exercise faith to trust in Him. He is the One "who opens our eyes to underlying spiritual realities." Without the Holy Spirit's miraculous intervention in our lives, we would have been doomed to an eternity of separation from God.

THE HOLY SPIRIT IMPARTS UNIQUE SPIRITUAL GIFTS TO US

When you were born physically, you were born with certain natural gifts and abilities. Some people were born with musical talent, others with the ability to work with their hands, and some with natural leadership skills. When you are born again, the Holy Spirit brings into your life a unique spiritual gift with which you can serve the kingdom of God.

> There are varieties of gifts, but the same Spirit.... But to each one is given the manifestation of the Spirit for the common good. (1 Corinthians 12:4,7)

The Holy Spirit gives some people the ability to speak God's Word clearly so as to bring conviction to listeners (prophecy); others are given the ability and desire to multiply their financial resources to further God's work (giving); and other Christians enjoy meeting the practical needs of people (serving) (see Romans 12:6-8).

It is no accident that the primary word the apostle Paul used to describe the unique spiritual gift the Holy Spirit brings into our lives is *charismaton*, which comes from the root word *char* meaning "joy." In my pastoral experience, I have never seen any one truth bring more joy and satisfaction into a Christian's life than the discovery of his or her spiritual gift. Realizing that God has given us a unique desire and power to fulfill a plan much larger than ourselves can revolutionize our lives. The late Ray Stedman once said that every morning when he awakened, he reminded himself of this thought:

> I am a part of the plan of God. God is working out all
> things to a great and final purpose in the earth, and I am
> part of it. What I do today has purpose and significance
> and meaning. This is not a meaningless day I am going
> through. Even the smallest incident, the most apparently
> insignificant word or relationship, is involved in His great
> plan. Therefore all of it has meaning and purpose.[6]

The Holy Spirit is the One who connects us to God's eternal purpose by giving us a unique spiritual gift.

THE HOLY SPIRIT SECURES OUR FUTURE

How can I know that once I trust in Christ for my salvation, I will keep on trusting Him? What guarantee do I have that God will keep His promises to me? How can I be sure that when I die, God will not leave my body (and spirit) in the grave? The answer to all of these questions is the Holy Spirit. He is our security for the future. Read the following promise carefully:

> In Him, you also, after listening to the message of truth, the
> gospel of your salvation—having also believed, you were
> sealed in Him with the Holy Spirit of promise, who is given
> as a pledge of our inheritance, with a view to the redemp-
> tion of God's own possession, to the praise of His glory.
> (Ephesians 1:13-14)

Here Paul used two words to describe how the Holy Spirit guarantees our salvation. First he described the Holy Spirit as a *seal*. In the Roman culture in which Paul lived, seals played a prominent role in everyday life. Today if you have an important document you want authenticated, you take it to a "notary" who will pull out a special instrument and impress your document with a raised seal and say, "That will be five dollars, please."

The notaries of Paul's day wore a special ring bearing the official insignia of the king or emperor. The official would press his ring on a seal of hot wax, transferring the insignia of the ring to the wax, securing the document as well as authenticating it. When a letter or public proclamation bore the official seal, it was recognized as carrying all the weight and authority of the king.[7] When we trust in Christ as our Savior, the King of kings stamps us with His Holy Spirit, assuring us that we really belong to Him.

Paul also referred to the Holy Spirit as a *pledge*. The Greek word actually means "down payment." The Spirit's presence within us is an absolute guarantee that one day God will take us to heaven.

To continue our car metaphor, let's suppose that I go to the dealership and spot that shiny new red Cadillac that I have desired for months. It is exactly the make and model for which I've been longing. The salesman and I haggle a bit and finally agree on a price. I ask him to hold the car for me while I discuss it with my wife. He replies, "It will take a one-hundred-dollar nonrefundable deposit for me to hold the car until tomorrow," so I fork over a hundred-dollar bill.

Later that evening, after getting a green light from my wife to make the purchase, I look through the newspaper and find the exact same car at another dealer for one thousand dollars less than the deal I've just made. What do I do? While I certainly would hate to lose the hundred-dollar deposit, it really is no big deal, considering the money I will save going for the lower price.

But suppose that instead of a hundred-dollar down payment, the salesman had required a ten-thousand-dollar nonrefundable deposit. What are the chances I will renege on my promise if I had put down such a large amount of my wealth? You can bet that after making such a substantial down payment, I would consummate the deal!

When you become a Christian, God promises to save your body, soul, and spirit. As a guarantee of that promise, He gives you a deposit. But instead of some inconsequential down payment that would allow Him to back out of the agreement if He so desired, God has given you His Holy Spirit. Since the Holy Spirit is God Himself, this means that God has deposited all of His wealth—His entire Being—in you! With an investment like that, God is not about to walk away from His promise!

AND SO MUCH MORE

Stop for a moment and think about what the Holy Spirit has already done for you: He has given you the ability to trust in Christ for the total forgiveness of *all* your sins; He has imparted to you a unique spiritual gift to allow you to actively participate in God's plan; and He serves as your absolute security for God's future promises. We don't have to beg, bargain, or barter with God for any of these benefits. They are ours the moment we trust in Christ. As Billy Graham writes, "This is the good news: We are no longer waiting for the Holy Spirit—He is waiting for us. We are no longer living in a time of promise, but in the days of fulfillment."[8]

But our salvation from sin, empowerment for service, and security for the future are not the limit of the Holy Spirit's work in our lives. While every Christian enjoys this "basic" package, some wonderful, powerful "options" also are available. Here are just a few:

- peace when the world around you collapses
- guidance when you are faced with a tough decision
- boldness when you need to speak the truth
- power when you need to say no to temptation
- joy when you lose all reason to hope

While the "basic package" requires no effort on your part because the Holy Spirit indwells you, the above options and more —so much more—are available only to those Christians who learn what we are going to discover in the next chapter.

Three

THE SECOND BLESSING

*What the Holy Spirit Wants to Do for You
(Even If You're Not Charismatic)*

Diane Palmer would never have imagined in a thousand years that her life would take the turn it has in the last twelve months.

Ever since she trusted Christ as her Savior at age ten, Diane and her parents had prayed that she would marry a strong Christian. And Roger certainly seemed to be the answer to their years of faithful intercession. During two years of dating and the first years of marriage, Roger had always taken the initiative in spiritual matters: praying together, insisting that the family attend church on Sunday mornings, and encouraging their young children in a Bible memory program. That is why Roger's announcement that he was leaving Diane for a woman he had met at work came as such a shock to everyone.

But in the six months since Diane and Roger's separation, Roger and his lover have parted ways. He and Diane have talked sporadically by phone or when he comes to pick up their daughter every other weekend. "Diane, I'm confused. I know the Lord wants me to come back home, but I'm just not sure I can. Please be patient with me."

Roger's pleas only exacerbate Diane's feelings of rejection and anger. *Not sure you can come home? What makes you think I would even want you back?* Not that she has ever verbalized those words, but she has fantasized about such an exchange many times.

That's not all Diane has fantasized about recently. Several weeks ago at one of her daughter's soccer games, Diane met Rick Davidson, a divorced father of a girl the same age as Diane's. They enjoyed sitting together during the game and engaging in some innocent flirtation. During the past few weeks Diane has found herself daydreaming about Rick, wondering what a more intimate relationship with him would be like. From some of Rick's comments and lingering looks, she has good reason to believe she is not alone in her curiosity.

Diane had dreaded this weekend for days. Her daughter was away at a school retreat and Diane had nothing—absolutely nothing—planned except to catch up on housework and maybe begin a new research report for work. When the doorbell rang at eight o'clock Friday evening, she was relieved by the interruption but surprised by the interrupter. Rick was standing at the door with a carry-out pizza and a rented video. "Since our daughters are away this weekend," Rick greeted her, "I thought it would be foolish for both of us to sit alone at home."

Somehow, Diane had sensed that this moment would arrive. She was both tantalized and frightened. After her husband's rejection, Diane was grateful that someone as handsome as Rick would come knocking on her door on a Friday night. But she also knew that what might happen that evening could destroy any possibility of reconciliation with her husband. Suddenly she remembered something she had heard her pastor say: "When the devil comes knocking at your door, he does not come wearing a red suit, carrying a pitchfork, and smelling of smoke. Instead, he will come in the form of the most appealing figure you have ever seen."

Standing on the front step, Diane summoned every bit of willpower she had and said, "Rick, thanks for stopping by, but tonight just isn't a good night." He walked away disappointed as she stood there stunned that she had been able to say no to something she really wanted. Where did that power come from?

Arnold Oliver is a deacon in our church. After retiring from his work as executive director of our state's highway department, he worked part time for a large consulting firm and enjoyed spending the remainder of his time traveling with his wife, Sue. Last April Sue was diagnosed with ovarian cancer and was told that she had only a few months to live.

A few hours after the doctor delivered the devastating news to the Olivers, I visited them in the hospital. After we talked about the doctor's report, Arnold said, "Pastor, I want to show you something." He pulled out his pocket calendar and began flipping through the pages, starting with the current month and flipping forward through the end of the year. "See these empty pages? They are going to stay that way. I am going to spend the next six months with my wife, and that means I will not be going to any meetings—including yours!" I glanced around Arnold's imposing frame to see Sue grinning from ear to ear.

Arnold kept his promise. Never have I seen a man minister more faithfully to his wife. He and Sue faced her impending death with unbelievable courage.

One morning in the late summer Arnold called me. "Pastor, I wanted you to know that Sue has gone home to be with the Lord." Just four hours later, Arnold received a call from the nursing home where his mother resided informing him that she, too, had died.

In the space of a few hours, he had lost the two most important women in his life. Yet through the ordeal, Arnold's faith was strong. Several days later at his wife's memorial service, Arnold stood before a huge congregation and offered a loving tribute to his wife, along with a resounding declaration of his faith in the goodness and the wisdom of God.

After the service, countless people exclaimed to me, "How in the world did Arnold find the strength to speak the way he did? I never could have done such a thing." Good question. Where *did* that kind of strength come from?

One day a few years ago I decided to go home for lunch. Why do I bother to report such a mundane event? Because I *never* go home for lunch. In fact, when I walked through the door that day, my wife was so startled to see me that she nearly jumped through the ceiling. She posed the usual questions. Was I sick? Had I been fired? No, I explained, I just wanted to come home.

She went back into the bedroom to finish some work while I entered the kitchen to fix a sandwich. There my preschool daughter Dorothy greeted me, making me glad I had decided to obey my inner impulse. While spreading the peanut butter across the slice of bread, I suddenly heard my daughter coughing. I ran over to see her grabbing her throat and turning red—then purple. I had heard of the Heimlich maneuver but had no idea how to perform it. So I pounded Dorothy on the back until an Oscar Meyer mini-wiener went rocketing across the room.

Dorothy had never choked on anything before, and I had never come home for lunch before. Yet for some reason I chose to go home that day. Was my impulse just a coincidence...or something more?

Empowered by the Spirit

Victory over temptation. Courage under pressure. Promptings within our spirit. What do these phenomena have in common? I believe they are just some of the evidences of the Holy Spirit's work in the lives of Christians fully committed to living in the Holy Spirit's power.

In our initial exploration of the crucial question, "How can I experience more of God's power in my life?" we began by reviewing what Christians already possess. The Holy Spirit—God Himself—comes to live within us the moment we trust in Christ as our Savior. The Bible refers to that event as the baptism with the Spirit. As we saw in 1 Corinthians 12:13, the baptism with the Holy Spirit

- is experienced by every Christian, not just a select few. Even the corrupt Corinthians experienced the baptism with the Spirit;
- occurs one time, not many times—Paul wrote that there is "one Lord, one faith, one baptism" (Ephesians 4:5); and
- results in our total possession of God's Spirit, not just a partial possession. The Greek word for *baptized* means "immersed," not merely sprinkled.

And yet even though every Christian is *indwelt* by the Spirit of God, it is evident that not every Christian is *empowered* by the Spirit. Just look at other believers—better yet, look at yourself—and that fact becomes obvious. The majority of Christians I know lead lackluster prayer lives, are enslaved by one or more unbreakable habits, cannot control their thoughts or their speech, feel bitter toward at least one person who has wronged them, and rarely think about God apart from Sunday mornings.

But there seems to be a remnant of believers who are different. It's not that they don't have the same struggles as other people, but somehow they seem to live above those struggles. Their lives are characterized by unquenchable joy in the face of sorrow, overflowing love in spite of attacks, and an unending desire to please God in spite of disappointing setbacks. They regularly experience miraculous answers to their prayers. When they speak, you sense that it is really God speaking through them. If you were facing a crisis in your life, they are the people you would ask to pray for you because they seem to possess a direct line to heaven. You know the kind of Christians I am referring to. In fact, I imagine such a person has already come to your mind.

What separates these Christians from the masses of other believers? Many of them will identify an experience beyond their initial conversion when they were empowered by the Holy Spirit. For some, this unique experience occurs at a specific point in time. The great evangelist D. L. Moody recounted such an experience in his life. Although he was obviously already a Christian and had enjoyed tremendous success as an evangelist, Moody felt there was something missing in his relationship with God. He cried out to God pleading for greater spiritual intimacy and power. God answered Moody's plea suddenly and dramatically:

My heart was not in the work of begging…I could not appeal. I was crying all the time that God would fill me with his Spirit. Well, one day, in the city of New York—O, what a day!—I cannot describe it; it is almost too sacred an experience to name. Paul had an experience of which he never spoke for fourteen years. I can only say that God revealed himself to me, and I had such an experience of his love that I had to ask him to stay his hand. I went to preaching again. The sermons were not different; I did not present new truths, and yet hundreds were converted. I would not now be placed back where I was before that blessed experience if you should give me all the world—it would be as small dust in the balance.[1]

Without being overly analytical, those of us who are interested in experiencing more of God's power in our lives need to answer a simple question about Moody's experience (and that of countless others). If a Christian has already received the baptism with the Holy Spirit, then what is this additional experience that so many Christians like Moody seem to experience?

Some people refer to this experience as *the baptism of the Spirit* or *the second blessing* or *the filling of the Spirit*. Regardless of what you label it, both the testimonies of other Christians as well as the teachings of the Bible indicate that indeed there *is* an additional experience with the Holy Spirit for us beyond our salvation.

But why do we need something more? If we receive all of the Holy Spirit at the moment of our salvation—if He indeed is part of the "basic package"—why should we seek after any additional experience with Him? R. A. Torrey used an interesting analogy to address that question:

> So it is clear that every regenerate man has the Holy Spirit. But in many a believer the Holy Spirit dwells away back in some hidden sanctuary of his person, away back of conscious experience. So just as it is one thing to have a guest in your house living in some remote corner of the house where you scarcely know that he is there, and quite another thing to have the guest taking entire possession of the house, just so it is one thing to have the Holy Spirit dwelling way back of consciousness in some hidden sanctuary of our being, and quite another thing to have the Holy Spirit taking entire possession of the house. In other words, it is one thing to have the Holy Spirit merely

dwelling in us but we not be conscious of His dwelling,
and quite another thing to be filled or baptized with the
Holy Spirit. So we may put it with perfect accuracy in this
way: Every regenerate person has the Holy Spirit, but not
every regenerate person has what the Bible calls "the gift of
the Holy Spirit," or "the baptism with the Holy Spirit," or
"the Promise of the Father."[2]

While I agree in general with Torrey's sentiment, I would disagree with his terminology. As we saw in the last chapter, every
Christian *does* have the baptism with the Spirit, which is the gift of
the Holy Spirit promised by the Father. But while every Christian
has been baptized with the Spirit, not every Christian possesses the
filling of the Holy Spirit. Although the filling of the Holy Spirit is
available to everyone, it is experienced only by some.

What Is the *Filling of* the Holy Spirit?

As you read through the New Testament, you will discover about
fifteen references to the filling of the Holy Spirit. The phrase seems
to be used in two distinct ways in the Bible.

Luke, author of the book of Acts, often used the phrase "filled
with the Spirit" to describe the baptism with the Holy Spirit that
occurs at salvation. For example, the phrase is used to describe the
long-awaited coming of the Holy Spirit to the apostles: "They were
all filled with the Holy Spirit and began to speak with other
tongues, as the Spirit was giving them utterance" (2:4).

The apostle Paul (formerly Saul, a persecutor of the church)
was filled with the Holy Spirit as a result of his conversion:

So Ananias departed and entered the house, and after laying
his hands on him said, "Brother Saul, the Lord Jesus, who

appeared to you on the road by which you were coming,
has sent me so that you may regain your sight and be filled
with the Holy Spirit." (Acts 9:17)

Cornelius, the Roman centurion, as well as his family and servants, were filled with the Holy Spirit when they trusted in Christ: "While Peter was still speaking these words, the Holy Spirit fell upon all those who were listening to the message" (Acts 10:44).

Thus, sometimes the Bible uses "the filling of the Holy Spirit" to describe the experience of Jesus Christ pouring His Spirit into a believer's life at the moment of salvation.

BEING CONTROLLED BY THE HOLY SPIRIT

But far more often, the Bible uses the words "filled with the Spirit" to describe the process of being *controlled by* the Holy Spirit.

The Bible often uses the Greek term *pleroo* to describe the filling of the Holy Spirit. The word is a nautical term referring to the filling of a ship's sails that results in the vessel's being carried along. When we are filled with the Holy Spirit, we are being controlled by the Holy Spirit. He is carrying us to His intended destination. You see the word *pleroo* being used this way in a number of passages in the New Testament. As you read these verses, simply insert the word *controlled* for *filled* or *full* and it makes perfect sense:

Jesus, full of [controlled by] the Holy Spirit, returned from
the Jordan and was led around by the Spirit in the wilderness. (Luke 4:1)

Therefore, brethren, select from among you seven men
of good reputation, full of [controlled by] the Spirit and
of wisdom, whom we may put in charge of this task.
(Acts 6:3)

But being full of [controlled by] the Holy Spirit, he
[Stephen] gazed intently into heaven and saw the glory
of God, and Jesus standing at the right hand of God.
(Acts 7:55)

The disciples were continually filled with [controlled by]
joy and with the Holy Spirit. (Acts 13:52)

Do not get drunk with wine, for that is dissipation, but be
filled with [controlled by] the Spirit. (Ephesians 5:18)

What Being Filled with the Spirit Means to You

From these few verses we can draw several conclusions about the
filling of the Holy Spirit in contrast to the baptism with the Holy
Spirit.

Being Filled with the Spirit Is a
Command, Not a Promise

Someone has noted that there are seven references to the "baptism
with the Spirit" in the Bible, and in none of those instances is the
experience commanded. Instead, the baptism with the Spirit is
what God does for each believer upon salvation.

By contrast, not every Christian is automatically filled with
(controlled by) the Holy Spirit, even though he or she has been
baptized with the Holy Spirit. We must continually choose
whether to be controlled by the Holy Spirit or by something else.
For example, have you ever been controlled by anger? You know
the experience. A coworker, mate, or child says something that just
ticks you off. A still, small voice within you says, *Hold your tongue,
control yourself.* But you just cannot let the comment pass; instead,

you unleash a torrent of angry words. When you are controlled by anger, you are not controlled by the Spirit.

While channel surfing with your remote control, have you ever come upon a scene that you know you should flip by, but it was simply too tantalizing to resist? When you are controlled by lust, you are not controlled by the Spirit. Just about every minute of every day we must decide whether to submit to the Spirit's control.

BEING FILLED WITH THE SPIRIT IS A CONTINUAL EXPERIENCE, NOT A ONE-TIME EVENT

While the Bible describes the *baptism with* the Spirit as a one-time event that occurs at the moment of our salvation, there is no once-and-forever *filling with* the Holy Spirit. Instead, yielding to the Holy Spirit's control and guidance is a day-by-day, moment-by-moment choice on our part.

Again, think of a sailboat traveling across the Atlantic Ocean. Does the wind come only one time and fill the ship's sails for the entire journey? Of course not. The wind comes for a while, then it subsides, and sometimes it even changes direction. In the same way, there is no single occurrence in which the Holy Spirit once and forever controls us for the remainder of our lives. Paul's command to "be filled with the Spirit" is in the present tense, denoting a continual action on our part.

I feel the need to pause here and address an issue that is causing unnecessary confusion and frustration among many Christians. Without intentionally offending any group of believers, we need to expose the error of what I call "deliverance theology." This is the idea that through some special experience I can be forever "delivered" from my struggle with sin. Some people sincerely seek to gain a once-and-for-all victory over drug addiction, anger, or pornography through a supernatural encounter with God, often erroneously labeled "the filling of the Holy Spirit." For a while they experience success, but sooner or later they find themselves mired in the same problem, defeated and disenchanted.

Let me say this as clearly as I know how: The Bible does not promise a one-time spiritual experience that will end your battle with sin. If there is such a thing, Paul never discovered it, because he went to his grave struggling with sin. "No matter which way I turn I can't make myself do right. I want to but I can't," he confessed in Romans 7:18 (TLB). Instead of searching for a once-and-for-all deliverance from the raging battle within, we need to surrender to the Holy Spirit's control each moment of every day.

Being Filled with the Spirit Is God's Desire for Every Christian, Not Just a Select Few

The famous and oft-quoted preacher Vance Havner used to say that the average Christian is so subnormal that when he becomes normal, everybody thinks he is abnormal![3] Fortunately for us, being filled with the Holy Spirit is not an experience reserved for a special class of superspiritual saints; it is a reality God wants *every* Christian to experience. Paul's command to "be filled" in Ephesians 5:18 is plural, not singular, indicating this is an experience for everyone in the church, not just a select few.

The Benefits of Being Filled with the Spirit

Making the daily, conscious choice to live under the guidance of God's Holy Spirit results in some real benefits for the Christian.

Before Christ's death and subsequent ascension into heaven, His disciples were openly distraught about His impending departure. They felt abandoned and even betrayed by the One in whom they had invested three years of their lives. But Jesus assured them that His temporary departure was really for their benefit:

I tell you the truth, it is to your advantage that I go away;
for if I do not go away, the Helper will not come to you;
but if I go, I will send Him to you. (John 16:7)

Sometimes it is easy for us to be a little jealous of the disciples. Think what it would have been like to have seen Jesus face to face! To not only talk with Him, but actually to have Him gaze into your eyes and talk to *you*. To see with your own eyes His miraculous works. To actually feel His arms around you when you are discouraged.

And yet Jesus told the disciples that they would experience something *even better* than His physical presence. After His departure, Jesus would send His Holy Spirit to actually live *within* them. The coming of the Holy Spirit was not just some cold, abstract piece of theological dogma to be studied; it was a personal reality to be experienced. The Holy Spirit would bring to the disciples a measure of joy, peace, and spiritual power they had never enjoyed before, even when they were in the presence of Jesus Christ.

And this same joy, peace, and power are available to you and me today!

I mention this only to remind us that while being filled with the Holy Spirit is a command, it is a command *for our benefit*. When I say to my oldest daughter, "Julia, come get your allowance," I am ordering her to do something, but it is obviously something for her benefit. If she were to refuse (which hasn't happened yet), I would not force the money into her hand. I want her to receive willingly the money I have for her. So it is with God's command to be filled with (controlled by) the Holy Spirit. If we refuse the command and choose to handle life under our own power, we forsake the wonderful strengths and attributes God has provided through His Spirit. But if we obey His command and embrace the Spirit's control and guidance, we experience at least four tangible benefits.

POWER IN TIMES OF TEMPTATION

In his wonderful book *Revolution Within,* Dwight Edwards asserts that most Christians (including me for a long period of time) tend to think of their salvation experience as we would a car wash: "You go in a filthy clunker; you come out with your sins washed away— a cleansed clunker."

It is true that when we are saved, our sins are washed away. But something more happens that many of us fail to comprehend. As Edwards writes,

> It's as if, right there between the power wash and power rinse cycles, a brand new engine was dropped into the car, plus entirely new wiring. Of course the old engine is temporarily left in, and we can choose (foolishly) to operate by it and to live like the clunker we were. But we don't have to—because of a revolution that's happened within us.[4]

I grew up in a very conservative church that faithfully taught God's Word. Nevertheless, the basic message I learned and believed for many years was, "When you become a Christian, you are forgiven of your sins, but your sin nature will still be present in your life. Thus you will never experience consistent victory over sin until you are freed from your sin nature, and that will only happen when you get to heaven." The unintended result of such teaching is a tolerance for sin and an acceptance of defeat as part of the normal Christian life. In fact, we have even created a special category for Christians who are consistently defeated by sin. We call them "carnal Christians" and give the impression that such a lifestyle, though not ideal, is certainly understandable because of the "old engine" that remains within us.

But contrast that attitude with Paul's declaration in Romans 6:

How shall we who died to sin still live in it? Or do you not
know that all of us who have been baptized into Christ Jesus
have been baptized into His death? Therefore we have been
buried with Him through baptism into death, so that as Christ
was raised from the dead through the glory of the Father, so
we too might walk in newness of life. (verses 6:2-4)

Paul said that the "normal" Christian experience is a new way
of living characterized by victory and holiness rather than defeat
and sin. Because of the Holy Spirit's power within us, we no longer
have to give in to lust, anger, greed, or bitterness. We have been
released to a "newness of life" never before possible. How do we
experience that kind of freedom? In Romans 6, Paul explained three
essentials for enjoying victory in times of temptation.

Know the Condition of Your "Old Engine"

The New Testament clearly teaches that every Christian has two
"engines"—two sets of competing desires within. The old engine is
sometimes referred to as the "old nature" or the "old self." When
we are born into this world, we come equipped with a set of desires
that naturally pull us away from God. When God says yes, our old
nature automatically says no, and when God says no, our old
nature answers yes.

When we are born again, God places a new "engine" inside us
that gives us both the drive (pardon the pun) and the power to
obey God. Thus we have two engines that are constantly at war
with each another, trying to pull us in two opposite directions.

Christians tend to go to one of two extremes in their attitude
toward their old nature. Some actually deny its existence. In one of
my former churches, a young leader argued with me constantly
about what he called "the myth of the old nature."

"Christians no longer have a sin nature," he would insist. "Romans 6 says that the old nature has been done away with."

One day my friend decided that he was tired of being married, so he deserted his wife and five children. His mistake was ignoring the reality of a civil war that rages within the heart of every believer—a war Paul described this way:

> But I say, walk by the Spirit, and you will not carry out the
> desire of the flesh. For the flesh sets its desire against the
> Spirit, and the Spirit against the flesh; for these are in oppo-
> sition to one another, so that you may not do the things
> that you please. But if you are led by the Spirit, you are not
> under the Law. (Galatians 5:16-18)

But an even greater mistake than denying our sin nature is to exalt it. Whenever we conclude that we are prisoners of our evil desires as long as we inhabit the earth, we give our old nature more credit than it really deserves.

What is the true condition of our sin nature? How much power does it really have over us? Consider Paul's explanation of what happens to our sin nature when we give our lives to Jesus Christ:

> Knowing this, that our old self was crucified with Him, in
> order that our body of sin might be done away with, so that
> we would no longer be slaves to sin; for he who has died is
> freed from sin. (Romans 6:6-7)

Our old nature has been crucified, Paul wrote. Not wounded, but *crucified*. Think about the horrendous ordeal a victim of crucifixion endures. Five-inch nails are driven through his hands and feet. Once the victim is secured to the cross, he has to pull himself up and down to catch a breath. Slowly, he dies of asphyxiation. Finally, a Roman spear is thrust through his side to finish the job. The victim is not just wounded, he is dead.

Paul used that imagery to describe what happened to our old nature when we became Christians. When he claimed that our "old engine" has been "done away with," Paul was not suggesting that it has been removed from us. It's still there, at war with our new engine. But its stranglehold over our lives has been broken. Something that has been crucified doesn't have much of a grip! Our old nature has only as much power over us as we choose to give it.

Consider the Power of Your "New Engine"

It is not enough just to understand the condition of our old nature. We also need to consider the power of the *new force* God has placed in our lives: "Even so consider yourselves to be dead to sin, but alive to God in Christ Jesus" (Romans 6:11).

The Greek word for *consider* was familiar to the biblical accounting world. It means "to accurately calculate your financial condition." For example, let's say you ask your accountant to give you an accurate appraisal of your financial situation. He says, "I have great news for you. After subtracting your liabilities from your assets, your net worth is $100,000." Thrilled by the news, you go out and purchase a new car. Unfortunately, your check bounces from here to the moon. Embarrassed, you ask your accountant what happened. "Well, you don't *really* have $100,000. You are actually $250,000 in the red, but I wanted to make you feel good about your situation."

Obviously, your accountant did not give an accurate picture of your financial condition.

I used to hear Bible teachers explain Romans 6:11 this way: "Whenever you face temptation in your life, imagine that you are free from sin, and then act that way." In other words, just engage in some spiritual positive thinking, and you can overcome sin. I never quite figured out how that worked and spent many years living in defeat until I understood what Paul meant by the word *consider* in this passage.

Paul is not telling us to just pretend we are free from sin in order to make us feel (and act) better. Instead, we are to act as if we are free from sin because we indeed *are* free from sin! That's the accurate calculation of our condition. The same Holy Spirit who raised Jesus Christ from the dead is operating in our lives right now, giving us all the "horsepower" we need to defeat sin.

Present Your Body to God

Once we know that the power of our old nature is destroyed and have accurately calculated the new power we possess, we are to start allowing godliness rather than sin to have the final say in our lives. (The word translated *reign* below means "umpire." The umpire in any contest always has the final say.)

> Therefore do not let sin *reign* in your mortal body so that
> you obey its lusts, and do not go on presenting the mem-
> bers of your body to sin as instruments of unrighteousness;
> but present yourselves to God as those alive from the dead,
> and your members as instruments of righteousness to God.
> (Romans 6:12-13)

How might Paul say it if he were writing to you and me today? I don't know, of course, but since he was rather direct in his writing, I can imagine him saying something like this:

"Stop filling your eyes with pornographic literature and Inter-net sites, and start filling your eyes with the truth of God's Word.

"Stop using your tongue to spread gossip and dissension, and start using your tongue to praise God and build up others.

"Stop allowing your feet to take you where you should not go, and instead use them to spread the gospel of Christ.

"Stop allowing your mind to be controlled by fear and anxiety, and start allowing it to be controlled by the peace of God.

"Stop allowing your appetites to destroy your life, and start bringing those appetites in line with God's desire for your life."

In our own power, we can do none of the above. But by the power of the Holy Spirit, we can do *all* of these things. John Stott has said that every Christian's biography is written in two volumes. Volume 1 is the story of my old nature, my old self before my conversion. Volume 2 is the story of the new self I become through the indwelling of the Holy Spirit. Volume 1 of my biography ended with the crucifixion of my old nature. I was a sinner, I deserved to die, and I *did* die in Christ. I received my deserved punishment by being joined together with Jesus Christ, who suffered the wrath of God.

But volume 2 opens with my resurrection. My old life is finished; my new life has begun. When Paul claimed that we have been raised "to walk in newness of life," he was not referring just to some future resurrection of our bodies. Instead, we are raised to a new quality of life that begins the moment the Holy Spirit comes into our life.[5]

OTHER PRACTICAL BENEFITS

Power in times of temptation may be the most important benefit of living under the guidance and control of the Holy Spirit, but it is not the only benefit. Let's look briefly at three other practical results of Spirit-controlled living.

DIRECTION IN TIMES OF CONFUSION

Several years ago I wrote a book on discovering God's will titled *Hearing the Master's Voice*. The point of the book was that God promises to give direction to His children. "My sheep hear My voice, and I know them, and they follow Me," Jesus said in John 10:27. But *how* does God speak to us? That's the real question for many Christians. Certainly He guides us through His Word, the counsel of others, prayer, circumstances, and even our own desires.

But whether the dilemma confronting us is the choice of a mate, a vocation, or a church, there comes a time when we must make a decision. Usually when decision time comes, we feel a pull in a particular direction. What is that inclination? In many instances, it is the leading of the Holy Spirit. Listen to what Jesus promised His disciples as He prepared to leave them:

> I will ask the Father, and He will give you another Helper,
> that He may be with you forever; that is the Spirit of truth,
> whom the world cannot receive, because it does not see
> Him or know Him, but you know Him because He abides
> with you and will be in you. I will not leave you as orphans;
> I will come to you. (John 14:16-18)

God has not left us alone in this world to fend for ourselves. In times of confusion we have a Helper—the Holy Spirit—who will give us the direction we need, not only in major decisions, but in minor ones as well.

Sometimes that direction comes even when we are not looking for it. Many years ago when I was a youth minister, I awakened early one Saturday morning and told my wife that I had a strong impression that I should check on one of the teenagers in our youth group. I felt funny about calling her so early on a Saturday morning, and I wasn't quite sure what I would offer as a reason for calling, but I dialed the number anyway. The phone rang and rang without any answer, for which I was grateful.

About an hour later I received a call from the girl's mother telling me that her daughter had been in a terrible automobile accident the night before and was in the hospital. Fortunately, she survived, but as I have looked back on that experience (and others like it), I have wondered what prompted me to make that phone call. I believe it was the Holy Spirit of God.

Over the years I have learned to obey those inner promptings we all have occasionally to

- write a note of encouragement to someone who has come to mind;
- voice something in a meeting that I would normally not say;
- make a phone call to someone I have not heard from in a while;
- change my travel plans for no better reason than an uncomfortable feeling I have; and
- stop what I am doing and pray for someone or something I cannot stop thinking about.

What many people label as "intuition" or "a sixth sense" is really the direction of the Holy Spirit who, like the wind that fills a sail, gives specific direction to our lives.

COURAGE IN TIMES OF DANGER OR OPPORTUNITY

Being controlled by the Holy Spirit also provides us with an unexplainable measure of courage in the face of danger or overwhelming circumstances.

Todd Beamer and at least three other passengers aboard United Airlines Flight 93 realized that their lives were soon coming to an end. But they were not about to allow the terrorists who had hijacked their plane to use the jetliner as a missile to destroy hundreds of innocent lives. Their story from the never-to-be-forgotten morning of September 11 has become a part of our nation's history and will be retold for generations to come.

Those heroic passengers formulated a plan to rush to the front of the airplane and try to overtake the terrorists, knowing that in doing so they might be sealing their own fate. Nevertheless, they determined that they would rather die in a field in Pennsylvania than on busy Pennsylvania Avenue in our nation's capital.

Todd Beamer called an air-phone operator on the ground and asked her to relay to his wife, Lisa, and his two sons how much he loved them. He then asked the operator to pray with him. After reciting the Lord's Prayer (including the phrase, "forgive us our trespasses as we forgive those who trespass against us"), the operator heard Todd utter those now immortal words to the other passengers: "Let's roll."

What gave Todd Beamer the strength to face death so courageously, to forgive those who were about to take his life, and at the same time fight them to the death in order to save hundreds of innocent lives? Todd was a dedicated Christian. I believe the Holy Spirit gave him inexplicable courage in the face of danger and death.

We see a vivid illustration of that same kind of courage in Stephen, the first Christian martyr. Stephen was a man described as being "full...of the Holy Spirit" (Acts 6:5). In spite of stiff opposition from the Jewish leaders, Stephen continued to proclaim the gospel of Christ. The Jews were powerless to stop him. Here's why: "They were unable to cope with the wisdom *and the Spirit* with which he was speaking" (Acts 6:10).

Finally, the religious leaders falsely charged Stephen with blasphemy and dragged him before the Sanhedrin, the ruling council of the Jews. But Stephen refused to be intimidated. Acts 7 records his sermon in which he boldly proclaimed that Jesus is indeed the Son of God. Notice how Stephen concluded his message to the

Jewish rulers: "You men who are stiff-necked and uncircumcised in heart and ears are always resisting the Holy Spirit; you are doing just as your fathers did" (verse 51).

This is not exactly the kind of message that wins friends (or acquittals). Stephen's charge sent the Jews into an absolute frenzy!

> When they heard this, they were cut to the quick, and they began gnashing their teeth at him. But being *full of the Holy Spirit,* he gazed intently into heaven and saw the glory of God, and Jesus standing at the right hand of God; and he said, "Behold, I see the heavens opened up and the Son of Man standing at the right hand of God." But they cried out with a loud voice, and covered their ears and rushed at him with one impulse. (verses 54-57)

The leaders drove Stephen out of the city and began stoning him. But even that could not silence this man who was "under the influence," so to speak, of the Holy Spirit: "Then falling on his knees, he cried out with a loud voice, 'Lord, do not hold this sin against them!' Having said this, he fell asleep" (verse 60).

Being controlled by the Holy Spirit gives us the courage to

- share Christ with an unreceptive audience;
- use adversity as an opportunity to display God's power; and
- face death with the assurance that something better awaits us.

COMFORT IN TIMES OF STRESS

Last night I visited a couple in our church who had just received some disturbing news. A few months ago the husband, who had never been sick a day in his life, discovered he has colon cancer. Over the last several weeks, he has been receiving chemotherapy treatment to reduce the size of the tumor. This past week he lost the vision in one of his eyes, suggesting that the tumor has metastasized into his brain.

I never know what to say in such circumstances. Any words I can offer seem hollow and trite. But last night I really didn't have to say anything. I just listened. "Yes, we are disappointed," they told me, "but we know God is still in control of the situation. We are just trusting Him to do whatever He thinks is best." They went on to describe the kind of funeral service they wanted me to conduct when the time came—a service that would glorify God and reach those who might not know Christ.

What is the source of such inexplicable peace? Again, the answer is the Holy Spirit. Jesus explained that another benefit of the Helper He would send would be a supernatural calm we can enjoy—even when the world around us is collapsing. "Peace I leave with you; My peace I give to you; not as the world gives do I give to you. Do not let your heart be troubled, nor let it be fearful" (John 14:27).

When that telephone call comes in the middle of the night telling us there has been an accident, when the doctor's report is not what we expected, when our mate announces he is leaving, or when our employer tells us we are no longer needed, we can experience a peace that surpasses all understanding (see Philippians 4:7). We can choose to be controlled by our circumstances, or we can be controlled by the still, small voice that encourages us to "Be still, and know that I am God" (Psalm 46:10, NIV).

Power in times of temptation. Direction in times of confusion. Courage in times of danger or opportunity. Comfort in times of stress. These are just a few of the limitless rewards of being controlled by the Holy Spirit.

But while these benefits are available to all, the fact remains that they are truly *experienced* only by a few. Why is that? What must we do—if anything—to experience this kind of supernatural power in our lives?

The answer to that question is the focus of the remainder of this book.

Four

WHAT GOD DESIRES FROM YOU

Why "Letting Go and Letting God" Will Let You Down

You know the drill. Your teenager asks for help on his math homework. Although you feel exhausted from the day's activities and still have more tasks to complete before bedtime, you agree to help. Before you know it, *you* are the one trying to decipher a complex algebra problem while your child is in the next room chatting online with a friend.

If you supervise other people, you probably have had the experience of giving one of your employees a task to fulfill, and when you later check up on the assignment, your employee says, "I put it aside because I didn't understand how to…" So you patiently explain how to solve the problem. A few days later your employee offers another excuse for not completing the job. With your own deadline approaching, you reason silently, it would be easier if you just did the task yourself. So you do!

Or maybe you receive a letter from your accountant in January reminding you that "April 15 is just around the corner," encouraging you to fill out the enclosed questionnaire to aid in the preparation of your tax return. So you spend most of a Saturday with a calculator and stacks of files, answering questions about earned income, deductions, losses, and gains. Suddenly it dawns on you: *Wait a minute. Why am I spending hundreds of dollars for an accountant when I'm the one doing all the work?*

If similar incidents have ever happened to you, you are a victim of "upward delegation." We become victims of upward delegation whenever we allow a subordinate to give a job back to us that belongs to him. We are guilty of practicing upward delegation whenever we give back to a superior a job that he has assigned to us.

In our spiritual lives, we are often the perpetrators of upward delegation—and God is the victim. We give back to Him assignments He has given to us.

For example, maybe a single mother in your small group at church mentions a specific request during prayer time. "My car recently lost its transmission, and I don't have the money for the necessary repairs. Without the car I can't get to work. Would you pray that God would provide the money for the repair work?"

So you pray aloud, "God, we know that You own the cattle on a thousand hills. Nothing is too hard for You. Please, Lord, answer our dear sister's request so that she can have a car and be able to provide for her family's financial needs. In Jesus' name, amen."

However, your small group really doesn't need God's help in the matter. Each person in your group has the ability to contribute at least fifty dollars to the cause; together you probably could cover the entire bill. But instead of passing the hat, you have collectively chosen to pass the responsibility to God. You have given Him a job that He already has given to you. Consider carefully what James wrote to his fellow Christians:

> If a brother or sister is without clothing and in need of
> daily food, and one of you says to them, "Go in peace, be
> warmed and be filled," and yet you do not give them what

is necessary for their body, what use is that? Even so faith, if it has no works, is dead, being by itself. (2:15-17)

Or maybe you have a family member who is not a Christian. For years you have been praying for his salvation: "Lord, please provide an opportunity for him to hear the gospel so that he might escape an eternity of separation from You." Tears stream down your face as you imagine your loved one engulfed in the flames of hell. Yet, in spite of your sincere interest in your family member's eternal future, you have never mustered up the courage to share the gospel with him. Instead, you've asked God to do the task that He has already assigned to you.

Sure, God could miraculously shout the Four Spiritual Laws from heaven or supernaturally switch the television program your loved one is watching from *Friends* to an evangelistic crusade. But God's preferred plan is for *you* to explain the way of salvation to your family member.

How then will they call on Him in whom they have not believed? How will they believe in Him whom they have not heard? And how will they hear without a preacher?… So faith comes from hearing, and hearing by the word of Christ. (Romans 10:14,17)

One more example. Frustrated with a mediocre spiritual life and hungry for something more in your relationship with God, you pray, "God, I am tired of living a life of continual defeat and disappointment. I need to experience Your power in my life. I'm tired of fighting by myself. If anything supernatural is going to happen, You are going to have to do it. Lord, fill me with Your Holy Spirit. I pray in Jesus' name, amen."

Have you ever prayed such a prayer? If so, you have once again practiced "upward delegation." When we ask God to fill us with the Holy Spirit, we are handing back to God a responsibility He has given to us.

In our attempt to answer the question, "What must I do to experience more of God's power in my life," some may legitimately ask, "Well, is there *anything* I can do to experience God's power in my life? After all, didn't Jesus teach that the wind of the Holy Spirit 'blows where it wishes'? To attempt to appropriate God's power in my life is nothing but spiritual manipulation. He alone is responsible for sending His power into my life."

First Things First

Before we examine our role in experiencing God's power in our lives, it is important to get a few key issues settled. Indeed, there are many tasks that only God can perform in our lives. For example, *regeneration* (the work of the Holy Spirit that gives us the ability to trust in Christ as our Savior) is something that only the Holy Spirit can do. When Jesus spoke to Nicodemus about the mystery of the Holy Spirit's working, He was referring to the Spirit's work of regeneration:

> Truly, truly, I say to you, unless one is born of water and the Spirit he cannot enter into the kingdom of God. That which is born of the flesh is flesh, and that which is born of the Spirit is spirit.... The wind blows where it wishes and you hear the sound of it, but do not know where it comes from and where it is going; so is everyone who is born of the Spirit. (John 3:5-6,8)

Another example of a work that only God can perform in our lives is our *justification*. This term refers to God's declaring us "not guilty" because of the death of Christ for our sins. When we trust in Christ as our Savior, God clothes us in His righteousness so that we are acceptable in His sight.

For example, men, imagine that you decide to treat your mate to dinner at an expensive and exclusive restaurant. You dress in nice, casual attire and arrive at the restaurant ready for a memorable evening. However, as you give your name to the maître d', he gives you the once-over and, with a condescending smile, says, "I'm so sorry, but our restaurant has a policy that requires you to wear a dinner jacket." You argue that you knew nothing of such a policy and had been looking forward to the evening for weeks. "No problem," he says. "We have an extra jacket that we will be happy to lend you."

At that moment you have a choice. You can either protest about the unfairness of the rule, stomp out of the restaurant, and miss a wonderful meal; or you can accept the maître d's offer, put on the jacket, and enjoy a memorable evening. The choice is yours.

The Bible says that none of us has the right "clothes" to enter heaven. Our righteousness—the best we can do—is like a filthy rag in the sight of God. But God offers to clothe us in the perfect righteousness of His Son Jesus Christ when we trust in Him for our salvation. It is that righteousness the apostle Paul desired, so that he might

> be found in Him, not having a righteousness of my own derived from the Law, but that which is through faith in Christ, the righteousness which comes from God on the basis of faith. (Philippians 3:9)

We can choose to reject God's offer and miss heaven, or we can humble ourselves, accept God's gift, and enjoy eternity with Him. The choice is ours.

Regeneration and justification are two works that God alone

performs in our lives without *any* assistance from us. But there is another work of God in our lives that does require our effort.

GOD'S WILL FOR YOUR LIFE

One thing most preachers learn after a while is that there are a few topics that will always guarantee a crowd. "Countdown to Armageddon" and "Six Secrets for a Scintillating Marriage" are obvious crowd pleasers. Another sure winner is "How to Know God's Will for Your Life." Most Christians are naturally interested in discovering the right job, the right mate, the right school, or the right answer to some dilemma.

Although the Bible does not answer all of our specific questions about God's direction for our lives, it does clearly answer the question, "What is God's will for my life?" Here it is:

> And we know that God causes all things to work together
> for good to those who love God, to those who are called
> according to His purpose. For those whom He foreknew,
> He also predestined to become conformed to the image of
> His Son, so that He would be the firstborn among many
> brethren. (Romans 8:28-29)

Far too often, Christians quote only the first half of the first sentence, ending with the word "good." If they run into difficulty, they comfort themselves with the thought that all things work together for good, meaning that they need to look for the silver lining in the cloud or wait patiently until they discover the reason for their difficulty. They believe that ultimately there will be that "aha" moment when they will be able to say, "*Now* I understand why I lost my job" or "*Now* I can see the good that came from my child's death."

But the problem with that kind of interpretation is that it's based on an erroneous definition of the word *good*. When we define *good* as "happiness, satisfaction, or understanding," we're going to end up disappointed with God. In reality, some things that happen to us are so painful that we may *never* see the good in them—not in this life, anyway.

Then what was Paul promising in Romans 8:28-29? Notice that he links the word *good* to the phrase *His purpose*. Paul assures us that every success as well as every failure, every triumph as well as every tragedy, is working toward God's purpose in our lives. And what is that purpose?

This may disappoint some people, but everything in life is *not* working together to

- make you successful in your career;
- give you a satisfying marriage;
- heal you of your disease; or
- provide you with financial security.

Instead, Paul said that the "good" for which everything in our lives is working is "to become conformed to the image of His Son." From the multitude of perishing humanity, God determined to save a group of people who would become just like His Son, Jesus Christ. Think of it this way. You and I were on spiritual death row, without any hope at all, awaiting our execution. But just when our situation looked bleakest, God walked down the corridor, stopped at some of the cells, and whispered something to those prisoners beyond our hearing. We could hardly believe what we saw next. God unlocked their cells, patted them on the back, and sent them out the door. They were free! Then He continued walking, past a few other prisoners, but He stopped at our cell door, looked into our eyes with love, and said, "I choose *you*."

> But God, being rich in mercy, because of His great love
> with which He loved us, even when we were dead in our

transgressions, made us alive together with Christ (by grace you have been saved). (Ephesians 2:4-5)

Think of it: God chose to save you for a purpose! His plan for your life goes far beyond rescuing your soul from hell. He wants to perform a spiritual "makeover" in your life so that you resemble Jesus Christ in your attitudes, affections, and actions. God desires that you think as Jesus thought, love what Jesus loved, and act as Jesus would act in every situation.

In theology, we use the term *sanctification* to refer to the process by which we become like Jesus Christ. The key term here is *process*. As someone once said, "Justification is the work of the moment, but sanctification is the work of a lifetime." Just as there was a year, month, day, and minute when you were born into this world, there is a precise time when you were born into the family of God. It happened the moment you trusted in Christ as your Savior. In that moment you were justified—declared "not guilty." But your "new birth" experience was not the end of God's working in your life; it was just the beginning!

Can you imagine a new mother in the hospital, after enduring nine months of pregnancy and the pain of childbirth, holding her newborn infant for a few minutes and then returning him to the doctor, saying, "That was nice. Tell him I love him and to have a good life"? Of course not! A baby's birth represents the beginning, not the end, of a parent's involvement with her child.

In the same way, our salvation is just the beginning of God's supernatural work in our lives. As Paul wrote to the Christians in Philippi: "For I am confident of this very thing, that He who began a good work in you will perfect it until the day of Christ Jesus" (Philippians 1:6).

God is not about to abandon you in the spiritual delivery

room. He regenerated you (gave you the ability to trust in Christ) and justified you (declared you not guilty) and baptized you (gave you His Holy Spirit) for a purpose: that you might become just like Jesus Christ in every area of your life.

Now here is the $64,000 question. If God alone is responsible for your regeneration, justification, and baptism with the Spirit, shouldn't you also assume that He is solely responsible for your sanctification—for conforming you to the image of His Son? Frankly, such a question has confounded and confused Christians for many centuries and has led to two extreme—and erroneous—ideas about our responsibility in sanctification.

THE PROBLEM OF PASSIVITY

I imagine at some point you have heard someone say, "You cannot live the Christian life by yourself. If you rely on your own strength, you are destined to fail. Instead, the key is to allow Jesus Christ to live His life through you. All you need to do is relax, let go, and let God do His work in you." Those advocating such a passive attitude toward the Christian life can point to some convincing passages in Scripture:

> I have been crucified with Christ; and it is no longer I who live, but Christ lives in me; and the life which I now live in the flesh I live by faith in the Son of God, who loved me and gave Himself up for me. (Galatians 2:20)

> Are you so foolish? Having begun by the Spirit, are you now being perfected by the flesh? (Galatians 3:3)

> Abide in Me, and I in you. As the branch cannot bear fruit of itself unless it abides in the vine, so neither can you

unless you abide in Me. I am the vine, you are the branches; he who abides in Me and I in him, he bears much fruit, for apart from Me you can do nothing. (John 15:4-5)

A vine does not have to struggle to produce fruit. As long as the sap flows freely from the vine through the branches, the fruit comes effortlessly. Jesus Christ is the vine, and we are the branches. As long as we allow the "sap" (a.k.a., the Holy Spirit) to flow through our lives, we do not need to exert any effort.

Or so the argument goes.

There are two major problems with this passive view of the Christian life.

First, *passivity denies the reality of my sin nature.* In chapter 3 we saw that when we are baptized with the Holy Spirit, we receive a new desire and ability to please God. Nevertheless, our old set of desires (the old "engine") is still present within us and struggles against our new nature. Paul described that civil war within himself:

I don't understand myself at all, for I really want to do what is right, but I can't. I do what I don't want to—what I hate. I know perfectly well that what I am doing is wrong, and my bad conscience proves that I agree with these laws I am breaking.... No matter which way I turn I can't make myself do right.... When I want to do good, I don't; and when I try not to do wrong, I do it anyway. (Romans 7:15-16,18-19, TLB)

Every time I read this passage, I feel as if Paul has been sneaking a peek at my spiritual journal. I imagine you feel the same way as well. You promise, "God, today I am not going to lose my temper," and within an hour a volcanic eruption of angry words spews from your mouth. Or you pledge, "Whatever else I do, I am going to start reading the Bible and praying every day," and by the end of the week, you find yourself back in the habit of watching sitcom reruns instead of spending time with God.

We need to understand that this kind of struggle is inevitable. There are no formulas, there are no "secrets," and there are no one-time experiences that will end the war raging between the "new you" who desires to please God and the "old you" who is at war with God. The Christian life is a struggle. Always has been, always will be.

But we also need to understand that this struggle is winnable. As we saw in chapter 3, our sin nature has no more power over our lives than we choose to allow it to have. Paul exclaimed:

> Thanks be to God that though you were slaves of sin, you
> became obedient from the heart to that form of teaching to
> which you were committed, and having been freed from sin,
> you became slaves of righteousness. (Romans 6:17-18)

Allow me to illustrate what Paul was saying. More than two hundred years ago, our forefathers came to this country. Nevertheless, they were still under the tyranny of England. Tired of taxation without any representation, they fought a revolutionary war to gain their independence from King George. Because of the courage and sacrifice of people like Patrick Henry, Thomas Jefferson, George Washington, and countless others, you and I enjoy freedom.

Now shift back to today and imagine that you receive a letter from the English government telling you that because of increased government expenses, Parliament is requiring you to send 10 percent of your income to the British treasury. How would you respond to such a notice?

You would probably toss it in your circular file. Why? You are under no obligation to a foreign government. Your forefathers gave their lives to provide you with freedom from the government of England.

In the same way, our spiritual forefather Jesus Christ gave His life to set us free from the power of sin. Although our old nature consistently tries to assert its authority over us, we have absolutely no obligation to obey it.

Not only does a passive view of the Christian life deny the reality of my sin nature, but *it also defers responsibility to God that He has given to me*. Remember the definition of *upward delegation?* "Giving to someone else responsibility he has given to us." God refuses to accept entire responsibility for our becoming conformed to the image of His Son. His Word makes it clear that we are to be actively involved with Him in the process:

> But I say, [*you*] walk by the Spirit, and you will not carry out the desire of the flesh. (Galatians 5:16)

> That, in reference to your former manner of life, *you* lay aside the old self, which is being corrupted in accordance with the lusts of deceit,…and [*you*] put on the new self, which in the likeness of God has been created in righteousness and holiness of the truth. (Ephesians 4:22,24)

> But now *you* also, put them all aside: anger, wrath, malice, slander, and abusive speech from your mouth. (Colossians 3:8)

> For if *you* are living according to the flesh, *you* must die; but if by the Spirit *you* are putting to death the deeds of the body, *you* will live. (Romans 8:13)

> And do not get drunk with wine, for that is dissipation, but [*you*] be filled with the Spirit. (Ephesians 5:18)

Starting to get the idea? "You walk," "you lay aside," "you put on," "you put to death," and "you be filled" are all commands directed at us, not God. To simply "let go and let God" is neither realistic nor biblical.

"If It's Going to Be, It's Up to Me"

The other extreme in the Christian life is equally futile and frustrating: the roll-up-your-shirtsleeves, pull-up-your-bootstraps, grit-your-teeth approach to sanctification. Discipline yourself to read three chapters of Scripture each day, pray regularly, attend church services, and abstain from certain sins, and presto—you will become like Jesus Christ.

Yet, without God's power surging through us, we are powerless.

During a recent Sunday morning sermon, I spread some dirt on our nice white carpet around the pulpit (you could hear the gasps). I then brought out a vacuum cleaner and asked the congregation, "How many of you believe that this vacuum cleaner is capable of cleaning up this dirt?" Everyone raised their hands. "Now, let me show you why you're wrong." I then pushed the vacuum cleaner over the dirt, and absolutely nothing happened. "Why isn't the vacuum cleaner doing its job?" I asked the congregation. One of my brighter members shouted out, "Because it's not plugged in!"

Exactly. Trying to remove the dirt in our lives so that we might become like Christ without plugging in to the power of the Holy Spirit is just as futile as trying to clean a stained carpet with an unpowered vacuum cleaner. As A. W. Tozer wrote, "The Spirit is an imperative necessity. Only the Eternal Spirit can do eternal deeds."

Everyone in the congregation nodded in agreement.

"Now, let me ask you another question," I continued. "How many of you believe the power of God is sufficient to clean up the sin in my life and make me like Christ?" Again, everyone agreed. "Now, let me show you why you're wrong again!" I then took an extension cord that was plugged in to an outlet, knelt down, and ran the other end of the cord over the dirt on the carpet. "As powerful as the electricity surging through this cord is, it cannot remove the dirt on this carpet by itself. It takes a vacuum cleaner plugged in to a power source to accomplish the job."

I then plugged the vacuum cleaner in to the power cord and began the cleanup work. Over the whir of the motor I said, "Only when the vacuum cleaner is plugged in to the power source can it do its work. In the same way, removing the sin of my life so that I can be like Christ is a cooperative effort between me and God. Without God, I cannot; without me, God *will* not."

The Purpose and Process of God's Power

In the remaining pages of this book, we are going to discover this cooperative process between God and us that guarantees the release of His supernatural power. But I want to conclude here with two statements that summarize what we have learned in this chapter about God's power.

First, *the purpose of God's power is transformation, not exhilaration.* We will say more about this later, but we need to be continually reminded that God's Spirit has one overriding purpose in our lives that has little to do with warm, fuzzy feelings in worship services, miraculous manifestations of His power, or even supernatural answers to prayer. God's singular purpose in our lives is to make us like His Son, Jesus, in our attitudes, actions, and affections.

Second, *the process by which we experience God's power is cooperation, not delegation.* While the baptism with the Holy Spirit is God's work alone, the filling by (or with) the Holy Spirit is a cooperative effort between God and us. We make a tremendous mistake when we think that we can manipulate or harness the power of the Holy Spirit. There is no formula or technique that guarantees His working. After all, He is a Person, not a force. He decides how and when He is going to operate. But that does not mean we simply sit back and do nothing. Instead, as J. I. Packer writes, we need to prepare the way for the Spirit's working:

> Prepare, in the sense of removing boulders from the road—obstacles such as habitual sins, neglect of prayer and fellowship, worldly-mindness, indulgence of pride, jealousy, bitterness, and hatred as motives for action.[1]

In the next four chapters we will discover four specific ways we can prepare the way for the supernatural working of God's Spirit in our lives.

Five

HOW TO TAKE A
SPIRITUAL BATH

Hint: It Takes Both Water *and* Soap

In his book *Seven Reasons Why You Can Trust the Bible,* Dr. Erwin Lutzer poses the following scenario. Imagine that you are in Los Angeles, California, and you find yourself late at night in a riot area of the city (which I did one Friday evening due to a series of wrong turns). Your front tire has gone flat, and you are sitting alone in your car figuring your next move. You look out your left window and see a gang of twelve young men leaving a nearby building and moving toward your car. Your whole life flashes in front of you as you imagine yourself being dragged from your car, beaten, robbed, and perhaps even killed.

Would it make any difference to you if you found out that these twelve men were leaving a Bible study on their way home?

As Dr. Lutzer explains, even the most hardened atheist would find some comfort in that information. Why? Even an unbeliever understands in a limited way the power of the Word of God to change lives.[1] Through Jeremiah the prophet, God said, "Is not My word like fire?…and like a hammer which shatters a rock?" (Jeremiah 23:29).

ARE WE MINIMIZING THE POWER OF GOD'S WORD?

Unfortunately, many Christians seem to have lost faith in the power of God's Word to transform lives. I see this lack of confidence in God's Word manifested in three specific ways.

"EVERYTHING BUT THE BIBLE"

One of the great cries of the Reformation was *"Sola Scriptura"*—the Bible alone. Yet in many churches today, the cry seems to be "Everything but the Bible!" I am not referring to churches and denominations that long ago rejected the inspiration and authority of the Scriptures. Have you noticed how little attention the Bible receives today in conservative, evangelical congregations that are otherwise willing to die for their belief in the inerrancy of the Scriptures? Donald Bastian wrote of this trend in a recent article in *Christianity Today:*

> I have seen the Bible given a less important place than it deserves in public worship. For example, my wife attended a service in the Midwest in which no Bible reading of any kind was a part of worship, and the preacher himself made casual mention of Scripture only a couple of minutes before the end of his sermon. My wife wondered if anyone else had noticed this glaring omission.
>
> An isolated case? A minister friend on vacation attended a congregation that advertised itself on the front lawn as a "Bible church." He was surprised that at no time was the Bible read except for a few verses before the pastor preached. While speaking to a denominationally diverse class at Northeastern Seminary in Rochester, New York, I asked, "How many of you lead or attend a church where

there is no separate Scripture reading as an act of worship?"
Nine of the 19 raised their hands.[2]

Not only is the public reading of Scripture absent in many congregations, so is the *teaching* of Scripture. Recently I had a Sunday off and was visiting my in-laws in another city. Early Sunday morning I was in the kitchen pouring coffee, and I turned on the television to check out the competition among my fellow television preachers (yes, we do that). I channel-surfed between three of my friends, all of whom have been a part of the conservative wing of our denomination that fights for the inerrancy of the Scripture. As I listened, I was dumbfounded by the scarcity of any reference to the Bible in their messages. Instead, they spoke on subjects such as "How to Develop Meaningful Friendships," "How to Have a Satisfying Marriage," and "Realizing Your Maximum Potential." There were few, if any, references to the Bible they had spent years defending.

THE RISE OF BIBLICAL ILLITERACY AMONG CHRISTIANS

In one of comedian Jay Leno's memorable "Jaywalking" routines in which he asks simple questions of people on the street, he challenged a young adult, "Name one of the Ten Commandments."

"God helps those who help themselves?" came the hesitant reply.

Jay continued, "Name one of the apostles."

No answer.

But when Jay asked the respondent to name the four Beatles, the answer came quickly: "George, Paul, John, and Ringo."[3]

Such biblical illiteracy is not limited to unbelievers (not to suggest that Leno's audience is composed entirely of pagans). For the last few years, Wheaton College has tested the biblical knowledge of incoming freshmen. These teenagers arrive from mainline Protestant denominations, are of above-average intelligence, and for the most part are devout Christians with a long history of involvement in the church. Yet, when asked about some of the significant characters and events of biblical history,

- one-third of the students could not place the following in the correct sequence: Abraham, the Old Testament prophets, the death of Christ, and Pentecost;
- fifty percent of the students could not sequence Isaac's birth, Moses in Egypt, Saul's death, and Judah's exile;
- one-third of the students could not identify Matthew as an apostle;
- one-third could not find Paul's travels in Acts; and
- fifty percent did not know that the Christmas story was in Matthew, or that the Passover story was in Exodus.[4]

(By the way, how would you have scored on such a test?)

Wheaton professor Gary Burge has asked youth leaders if they are teaching their students the great stories of the Bible and the great doctrines of the faith. One answered, "It is hard to find time. But I can say that these kids are truly learning to love God." Burge writes,

> That is it in a nutshell. Christian faith is not being built on the firm foundation of hard-won thoughts, ideas, history, or theology. Spirituality is being built on private emotional attachments.[5]

MY OWN MINISTRY

Lest you think I was a little sanctimonious in describing some of my contemporaries' lack of emphasis on the Bible, I confess that it has been easy for me to fall into the same trap in an attempt to be "relevant" and "needs-oriented." Michael Horton's analysis of the contemporary Christian culture has caused me to do some serious reevaluation of my own ministry:

> We speak of peace of mind, emotional healing, recovery, dysfunction, self-talk, self-esteem, and so forth the way previous generations used to speak of original sin, atonement, justification, sanctification, and related biblical truths. Rather than a definitive source for all that we believe and teach, the Bible, in our present context, becomes a source of quotations for sermons and books that are essentially secular in their basic content and message. Just as the Bible was used to justify one philosophical school over another in the Middle Ages, in our day it is shaped like a wax nose to suit the latest fad.
>
> The problem is that this happens in churches that claim fidelity to the inerrancy of Scripture. The unfaithfulness is difficult to mark objectively, since there is a high view of Scripture in theory, whatever the practice. While liberals of various stripes undercut biblical authority by direct assaults, evangelicals of various stripes are today undermining biblical authority by claiming one thing in theory (the authority of an inerrant Bible) while in practice giving priority to secular disciplines and popular culture in defining and shaping the spiritual diet.[6]

All I can say to that is "Ouch!"

THE INCREDIBLE POWER OF GOD'S WORD

Let's turn the spotlight away from others and focus on you for a moment. Does God's Word have a prominent place in your life (not on your bookshelf, but in your *life*)? To help you formulate an honest and accurate answer, here are four questions to ponder:

1. During the past seven days, how much time have you spent thoughtfully reading the Bible—not books or devotionals about the Bible, but the Bible itself?

2. Could you explain to someone how to become a Christian using no tracts, booklets, or books other than the Bible?

3. If you found yourself in a prison cell or marooned on an island, how many verses of Scripture would you be able to recall from memory to provide emotional and spiritual comfort and strength?

4. If someone were to ask you for advice, would you know where to direct them in God's Word for help in resisting temptation, dealing with bitterness, handling a rebellious child, or experiencing peace of mind through life's storms?

The purpose of this quiz is not to heap guilt on your shoulders. I simply want to expose a major reason why we may not be experiencing more of God's power. His Word is the *primary* conduit through which His Spirit flows through our lives. Consider what God's Word is capable of doing.

THE POWER TO SAVE

Someone once asked G. K. Chesterton, "If you were marooned on a desert island and could have only one book, which would you choose?" Known for his strong Christian beliefs, he was expected to reply, "The Bible." Instead, Chesterton answered, "*Thomas' Guide to Practical Ship Building.*" Smart man! As author John Ortberg points out,

> That makes sense… When we're trapped on an island, we want a book that will help us get home. We don't want to be entertained or even informed. We want a book that will show us how to be saved.[7]

For the spiritually shipwrecked, the Bible is such a book. We were all trapped on an island of sin and desperately needed a way to return home to the Father who loves us. Only the Word of God provides the direction we need to get to heaven. While people may be drawn to the gospel by a song, a testimony, or a warm, fuzzy story, the Holy Spirit uses the Word of God to bring about new life. As James wrote, it is the "word implanted, which is able to save your souls" (James 1:21).

THE POWER TO GUIDE

Are you facing a monumental decision for which you need specific direction? God promises, "I will instruct you and teach you in the way which you should go; I will counsel you with My eye upon you" (Psalm 32:8).

But the real question for most of us is not, "Can God direct us?" but "*How* does God direct us?" The primary means—not the only means—by which God guides us is through His Word. Psalm 119 was a song written to affirm the sufficiency of God's Word for everything we need in life. Each of the twenty-two stanzas in this song begins with a different letter of the Hebrew alphabet. This was the psalmist's way of saying, "God's Word has everything you need in life from A to Z."[8] One of those many benefits of God's Word is the promise of guidance: "Your word is a lamp to my feet and a light to my path" (Psalm 119:105).

Have you ever walked along an unfamiliar path in the middle of nowhere without the aid of any illumination except a flashlight? A flashlight allows you to see a few feet—not a few miles—ahead of you. It provides just enough light so that you can see clearly to take the next step.

In the same way, God rarely provides us with enough light to see every step we need to take in the future (perhaps so that we are not tempted to run ahead of Him). But He promises to give us enough direction to take the *next* step. This is why the psalmist says that God's Word is a "light," not a "floodlight" to my path.

THE POWER TO HEAL

World history tells the story of Gordius, who tied a knot with such complexity that no one could figure out how to untie it. Then along came Alexander the Great, who realized he could never unravel the knot. So he pulled out his sword and sliced the knot in two.[9]

Sin is like a rope or a chain that enslaves us. We mistakenly think that disobedience to God will lead to happiness and freedom. It doesn't. Sin always results in misery and slavery, and the beginning point for sin is the mind. Wrong thinking leads to wrong behavior.

We think we are responsible for our own well-being, so we are bound up with anxiety, fear, and worry.

We think money is the key to happiness, so we are bound up in greed.

We think faithfulness to our mate will lead to boredom, so we are bound up in immoral thoughts, habits, and actions.

We think revenge is the best response to mistreatment, so we are bound up in bitterness.

We can spend years trying to free ourselves from those knots through counseling, books, seminars, or New Year's resolutions. Or, we can allow the sword of God's Word to slice through those enslaving thoughts and set us free. It is no accident that the writer of Hebrews described the Word of God as

living and active and sharper than any two-edged sword,
and piercing as far as the division of soul and spirit, of both
joints and marrow, and able to judge the thoughts and
intentions of the heart. (4:12)

The Roman two-edged sword was one clean, mean, killing machine! Unlike the double-bladed razor I shaved with this morning with two blades on one side, the two-edged sword was sharp on both sides. When a Roman soldier sliced someone in one direction, he would then flail the sword in the opposite direction and finish the job.

Yet God's Word is more lethal than the two-edged sword (not to mention my Gillette Atra razor) because it has the power to pierce to the very heart of who we are. That is not an easy job, given our limitless ability for self-delusion. As the prophet Jeremiah said, our hearts are deceitful, wicked, and cannot be trusted (see Jeremiah 17:9). Only the Bible has the ability to reveal our true motives for teaching a Bible-study class, fixing a meal for a bereaved family, running an errand for our mate, or writing out a check for a church project.

But God's purpose in slicing us open is not to hurt us, but to heal us. Through the healing power of His Word, God is the surgeon who cuts His patient open in order to remove the cancerous tumor of sin that is destroying his life. Dr. Lutzer says it this way:

> Our problem is that we want vitamins, not a knife…
> We want healing without the incision, the joy without the
> sorrow. But God gives us both. For the more thorough
> our repentance, the greater the infusion of grace. The more
> helpless we see ourselves to be, the more helpful God
> becomes. Surgery precedes recovery.[10]

As God Himself said, "See now that I, I am He, and there is no god besides Me; it is I who put to death and give life. I have wounded and it is I who heal, and there is no one who can deliver from My hand" (Deuteronomy 32:39). The Great Physician uses the scalpel of His Word to expose sin and bring healing to our lives.

THE POWER TO TRANSFORM

Warning to all English teachers: I'm about to commit the unpardonable sin of switching metaphors. Imagine that you have been working in the yard one July afternoon in one-hundred-degree heat. When you are through, you can't wait to jump into the shower and feel the grime being washed away from your body. You turn on the hot water, close your eyes, reach for the soap…only to discover that there is none. How do you feel (besides furious at the person who forgot to replace the soap)? Shortchanged, I'm sure. No one who is serious about hygiene would ever think of showering without soap. It takes both water *and* soap to cleanse us thoroughly.

Paul used a similar image in Ephesians 5 to describe what God desires for every believer:

> That He might sanctify her, having cleansed her by the
> washing of water with the word, that He might present
> to Himself the church in all her glory, having no spot or
> wrinkle or any such thing; but that she would be holy
> and blameless. (verses 26-27)

Remember that God's overriding purpose in our life is to transform us into the image of Jesus Christ. How does God remove the grime of sin that mars the image of His Son? With water *and* soap. He combines the "washing of water" (a frequently used description of the Holy Spirit) and "the word" (a reference to Scripture) to transform our actions, attitudes, and affections into those of His Son.

Unfortunately, some Christians rely exclusively on either the Bible or the Holy Spirit for this transformation. For example, we all know Christians who mistakenly equate biblical knowledge with spirituality. These are the kind of people who study the Bible as if they are preparing for a final exam, believing that when they reach the pearly gates, God is going to hand them a blue book and ask them to list ten evidences of the virgin birth of Christ or draw a chart explaining the end times! They view the Bible as a source of information, not transformation. Depending on the Bible without the Holy Spirit to "morph" us into the image of Christ is just as futile (and unsatisfying) as showering with a bar of soap and no water. Not a pleasant experience!

However, at the other extreme are those who view the Christian life as a series of fresh, usually emotional encounters with the Holy Spirit. They are continually chasing after new experiences, revelations, and supernatural manifestations without any consistent exposure to God's Word. Such an approach to the Christian life is like showering without soap. It leaves one wet, but not clean. Only the Spirit of God combined with the Word of God can transform us into the image of God.

Give God's Word the Prominence It Deserves

I am going to make an assumption about you that may or may not be true—but I have a hunch it is. I imagine that you can point to a time in your life when you read and studied the Bible more than you do today. How do I know that? Because I'm guessing that your reason for reading this book is a genuine desire to renew an intimacy with God that may have faded over the years. You may assume that your eroding interest in the Bible has been the natural result of your deteriorating relationship with God. If only you could recapture the excitement of your early Christian walk, you think, then you would have a fresh desire to invest time in God's Word as you used to.

But in reality, the opposite is true. The first key to experiencing more of God's power in your life is to renew your commitment to making the Word of God central in your life. How do you pull that off?

John Kass, a columnist for the *Chicago Tribune,* wrote a column about a waiter named Bouch who works at a tavern in Chicago. Bouch decided to write a letter to the king of his homeland, Morocco. King Mohammed VI is an extremely popular king because of the manner in which he freely interacts with his subjects in public. When Bouch wrote to the king from Chicago, King Mohammed VI wrote back. "Look at the letters," Bouch exclaimed to the newspaper reporter. "These are letters from the king. If I meet him, I'll be so happy."

Kass reflected, "How many guys hauling beer and burgers in a Chicago tavern have a correspondence going with a royal monarch?" The reporter interviewed Morocco's deputy counsel general in Chicago about the correspondence and was told that it was not unusual for the king to write personal letters to his subjects abroad. "It happens a lot," the official said. "The king loves his subjects."[11]

The King of the Universe loves His subjects even more! And as proof of that love, He has revealed everything we need to know about Him in the Holy Bible. However, before we will ever give the Bible the prominence it deserves in our lives, there are two key issues we must settle in our minds.

THE TRUSTWORTHINESS OF GOD'S WORD

First, we most be convinced of the trustworthiness of the Bible. How do I know that the Bible really is the Word of God? Certainly, we need to consider what the Bible says about itself. The apostle Paul wrote that "All Scripture is inspired by God…" (2 Timothy 3:16). The word that is translated *inspired* literally means "God-breathed." Every word in the Bible came from the mouth of God, and as my former pastor used to say, "God doesn't have bad breath!"

But beyond what the Bible claims for itself, are there any objective reasons for believing in the trustworthiness of the Bible?

I could devote the rest of this book to citing the historical, scientific, and archaeological evidence for the divine inspiration of the Bible. Since that is beyond the scope of our visit together, let me cite just one strong piece of evidence for the uniqueness of the Bible: its unity of theme. F. F. Bruce explains it this way:

> The Bible, at first sight, appears to be a collection of literature—mainly Jewish. If we enquire into the circumstances under which the various Biblical documents were written, we find that they were written at intervals over a space of nearly 1400 years. The writers wrote in various lands, from Italy in the west to Mesopotamia and possibly Persia in the east. The writers themselves were a heterogeneous number of people, not only separated from each other by hundreds of years and hundreds of miles, but belonging to the most diverse walks of life. In their ranks we have kings, herdsmen, soldiers, legislators, fishermen, statesmen, courtiers, priests and prophets, a tent-making Rabbi and a Gentile physician, not to speak of others of whom we know nothing apart from the writings they have left us. The writings themselves belong to a great variety of literary types. They include history, law…religious poetry…parable and allegory, biography, personal correspondence, personal memoirs and diaries, in addition to the distinctively Biblical types of prophecy and apocalyptic.
>
> For all that, the Bible is not simply an anthology; there is a unity which binds the whole together.[12]

The only explanation for the unity of theme and symbols you find in the Bible—a book written by more than forty authors (most of whom did not know one another) over a period of fourteen hundred years—is that it is a supernatural book.

THE COMPLETENESS OF GOD'S WORD

In addition to the trustworthiness of the Bible, we must also be convinced of the completeness of the Bible.

Imagine that your mate goes on an extended trip out of the country. There is no phone service where your spouse is, and after a few days (or weeks), you begin to miss him or her terribly. To console yourself you retrieve an old box from the garage filled with love letters from your mate that date back to your college days. While reading those letters you hear the doorbell ring. When you open the door you see the FedEx delivery man with a letter from your spouse. What would you do next? Would you continue reading those dated love letters, or would you set them aside and rip open the FedEx envelope?

A growing number of Christians are being led to believe that the Bible is like an old love letter, that even though it may contain sweet and authentic communication from God, it is nevertheless inferior to the "fresh words" God is speaking to the church today.

Does God speak to us today apart from the Bible? Is He revealing "fresh" truth about Himself not contained in the Scriptures? Again, we must consider what the Bible itself says. The New Testament writer Jude encourages us to "contend earnestly for the faith which was once for all handed down to the saints" (Jude 3). The Greek word translated *handed down* is written in a tense describing an activity that is *completed*. God has finished depositing all the truth we need to know about Him in the Bible.

Similarly, the apostle Peter promises that God has already "granted to us everything pertaining to life and godliness" (2 Peter 1:3). Those who have the Spirit of God in their hearts and the Word of God in their hands have everything they need to experience the power of God in their lives!

"Robert, are you saying that the only way God gives us direction is through the Bible?" Not at all. God can lead us through prayer, signs and circumstances, wise counsel, and even our own desires. Yet we should realize that any revelation from God we claim to receive apart from the Bible is subjective, and therefore subject to error.

Pastor Bob Russell tells about a young preacher who came to his church when Bob was growing up. The preacher was arrogant and hardly referred to the Bible during his message. After the service, Bob's mother approached the young minister and offered this word of advice: "Whenever you preach, always use a lot of Scripture, because that's one thing you know is true."[13]

As long as we are constantly searching for new revelation from God, we are in danger not only of being misled but also of missing out on what God is trying to say to us through His Word. One writer has explained it this way:

> Moreover, the promise of such [extrabiblical] guidance
> inevitably diverts attention from the Scriptures, particularly
> in the practical and pressing concerns of life. Let us never
> underestimate just how serious this diversion really is. In the
> Bible the church hears God's true voice; in the Scriptures,
> we know that He is speaking His very words to us. Advo-
> cates of words "freshly spoken from heaven" should beware:
> By diverting attention from the Scriptures, they quench the
> Spirit who is speaking therein.[14]

COMMIT TO QUALITY TIME IN GOD'S WORD

When I visit the family of someone who has died, I often ask to see the Bible of the deceased. More often than you might believe, the family has difficulty even locating the Bible. And in the event that the Bible is retrieved, the embarrassing crackling sound that accompanies its opening gives the distinct impression that this is a book that has been rarely used.

It's not that the dearly departed didn't believe in the Bible. He or she just rarely got around to reading it. Indeed, one survey revealed that while over 82 percent of Americans believed that the Bible was the "inspired Word of God," only about half read it at least once a month. Yet, of those who claimed to read the Bible at least once a month, 50 percent could not name one of the four gospels or identify the person who delivered the Sermon on the Mount.[15]

If God's Word is the primary tool the Holy Spirit uses to produce miraculous changes in us, then it only makes sense that we should commit to a regular program of Bible reading and study. Such a commitment requires *discipline*. I've heard many definitions of discipline, but my favorite is this one: "Discipline is doing what you know you should do even when you don't feel like doing it."

I don't want to shock you, but even though I'm a man of the cloth, there are many times I don't feel like reading the Bible. The newspaper, a phone call, or the late movie on American Movie Classics sometimes (make that *many* times) is much more alluring than a few chapters of Habakkuk. Yet I learned a long time ago that if I wait until I feel like reading the Bible, I could go longer than I would ever want to admit without opening it.

Remember, it is easier to act yourself into a feeling than to feel yourself into an action. Gordon MacDonald describes the role of spiritual discipline this way:

> Discipline is that act of inducing pain and stress in one's life in order to grow into greater toughness, capacity, endurance, or strength. So spiritual discipline is that effort pressing the soul into greater effort so that it will enlarge its capacity to hear God speak and, as a result, to generate inner force (spiritual energy) that will guide and empower one's mind and outer life.[16]

But beyond discipline, we also need *a plan* to follow in reading God's Word. It's up to you whether you choose to read through the Bible in a year or select one book of the Bible on which to focus for an entire month or follow some other program for reading the Bible. Regardless of your particular plan, let me share some ideas that can help your discipline and enhance your plan.

DESIGNATE A SPECIFIC TIME EACH DAY

You'll find it extremely helpful to designate a period of time each day in which Bible reading and study is your top priority.

Personally, mornings just don't work for me. Before work I am trying to help Amy get our children to school. Once I arrive at work, I'm so busy trying to prepare a message for others that I don't have time to reflect on what God's Word is saying to me (yes, I see the irony). I have discovered that after the kids have gone to bed in the evening is the best time for me to read and meditate on God's Word. Your schedule may be completely different. All that really matters is that you reserve *some* period of time in your day that's devoted to God's Word.

TRY A FRESH TRANSLATION

It's possible that you have read the same passage so many times in your favorite Bible that you find yourself simply going through the motions while your mind is somewhere else. Or as you read the passage, a note you wrote years ago in the margin of your Bible reminds you of a sermon, an event in your life, or a theological argument you had…and once again your thoughts begin to drift.

A pastor friend of mind gave me a great suggestion that has helped me overcome the "familiarity" problem. Each year, purchase a new translation of the Bible—not for study and note taking, but for your devotional reading. Consider using the *New King James Version, The Message,* the *New Living Translation,* or some other version of God's Word to allow God to communicate familiar truths in a fresh way.

You may be thinking, *Robert, you're a pastor. You're paid to read and teach the Bible. But I just don't have time. I have too many responsibilities rushing at me right now.* Gordon Gilkey has identified a popular misconception that we all have about our time. He says that we imagine ourselves standing in the middle of a large circle filled with tasks, problems, and responsibilities rushing at us at the same time. No wonder we feel so overwhelmed and exhausted! But Gilkey says that such a picture is simply a myth. Instead, he offers a more accurate comparison:

> What is the true picture of your life? Imagine that there is an hourglass on your desk. Connecting the bowl at the top with the bowl at the bottom is a tube so thin that only one grain of sand can pass through it at a time.
>
> That is the true picture of your life, even on a superbusy day. The crowded hours come to you always one moment at a time. That is the only way they can come. The day may bring many tasks, many problems, strains, but invariably they come in single file.[17]

The Christian who says, "I just don't have time to read the Bible" is only fooling himself. More tragically, he is really saying, "I am content with a mediocre spiritual life."

CONCENTRATE ON SMALLER SECTIONS OF THE BIBLE

My friend and seminary professor Howard Hendricks says he has encountered Christians who proudly proclaim, "I have read through the Bible fifty times." Hendricks's reply is, "The real question is not 'How many times have you been through the Bible?' but 'How many times has the Bible been through you?'" Remember, the goal of reading the Bible is not the completion of a task, but the transformation of your life. That is why it is far better to read a smaller section than to rush through a large section just to finish an arbitrary "Read Through the Bible in a Year" program.

Madame Guyon wrote,

> If you read [the Bible] quickly, it will benefit you little. You will be like a bee that merely skims the surface of a flower. Instead, in this new way of reading with prayer, you must become as the bee who penetrates into the depths of the flower. You plunge deeply within to remove its deepest nectar.[18]

LISTEN FOR—AND FOLLOW—GOD'S COMMANDS

What is the "nectar" that Madame Guyon said we should search for in God's Word? It is the timeless principles that apply to our lives. We need to be careful here. Some people mistakenly try to force any passage they read into a direct application for their specific dilemma. For example, one man was trying to determine which branch of the armed forces he should join. He flipped through his Bible and came to Psalm 107:23: "Those who go down to the sea in ships, who do business on great waters." That's all the direction he needed to enlist in the United States Navy![19]

Obviously, the purpose of Psalm 107 is not to help us choose between the army, air force, navy, or marines. The timeless truth in this psalm is that we should continually express gratitude to God in whatever situation we find ourselves: "O give thanks unto the Lord; for he is good: for his mercy endureth for ever" (verse 1, KJV). Why should we give thanks to God? Because He pours out His power and goodness to everyone, including those who do their business on the ocean.

Whether we are reading a chapter, a paragraph, or simply a verse of Scripture, we need to ask God to reveal any timeless truths that apply to us.

Then we need to go one step further. After we discover the timeless principle from the passage we are reading, we should develop a step of action to apply that principle. Again, if the goal of the Holy Spirit's work is to transform us into the image of Christ, then we should never close our Bible without answering the question, *What am I going to do differently because of the truth I have just encountered?*

For example, men, after reading Ephesians 5:25—"Husbands, love your wives, just as Christ also loved the church and gave Himself up for her"—you may identify this timeless principle from the passage: *I am to love my wife just as selflessly as Christ loves me.* Congratulations! You have discovered a great truth. But truth without transformation is empty knowledge that only "puffs up," as the apostle Paul once said. You need to take the additional step of answering the question, *How can I apply this truth in my life?* Perhaps demonstrating sacrificial love for your wife translates into agreeing to take the children to school in the morning, giving her a few nights off from preparing meals, or spending a day with her at the mall (on second thought, no need to go overboard!).

As you read God's Word, always keep in mind that your goal is not information, but transformation—becoming like Jesus Christ in your actions, attitudes, and affections. Along these lines, author John Stott offers a good reminder:

> If we come to the Scriptures with our minds made up,
> expecting to hear from it only an echo of our own thoughts
> and never the thunderclap of God's, then indeed he will not
> speak to us and we shall only be confirmed in our own
> prejudices. We must allow the Word of God to confront us,

to disturb our security, to undermine our complacency and
to overthrow our patterns of thought and behavior.[20]

Overthrowing our patterns of thought and behavior. That is
the kind of radical transformation that can only be accomplished
by the Spirit of God working through the Word of God...the
washing of water with the Word.

Six

THE POWER OF FAITH
KNEELING

Jabez Gibberish or Genuine Prayer?

"This book will revolutionize your life," Jerry promised as he handed the small volume to Don after their monthly men's breakfast. The book, less than a hundred pages long, told the story of an obscure figure from the Old Testament who prayed a simple prayer that resulted in God's supernatural blessings in his life.

"I have been following the principles in this book for the last month, and you just wouldn't believe all that has happened!" Jerry went on. "I received an unexpected raise at work, Shelia's and my marriage has improved dramatically, and my eighty-year-old father prayed to receive Christ last Tuesday evening."

Don had read about the book in *Newsweek* magazine and was naturally skeptical of any book that was so widely acclaimed by both Christians and non-Christians. A prayer asking God to "bless me" and "enlarge my border" sounded like a thinly veiled version of the name-it-and-claim-it theology of a few decades ago. Not only that, but Don was bothered by those who advocated praying this prayer verbatim once a day for thirty days. Didn't Jesus warn against formulaic prayer and meaningless repetition?

In spite of these initial reservations, Don read the book, more out of curiosity than anything else.

The book was much better than Don expected. The author clearly stated that "God's blessings" had little to do with a large salary or a new BMW. Instead, the writer explained that asking God to bless us was in effect saying, "God, I want nothing more, but nothing less, than what You desire for me." He observed that the main reason we are not experiencing God's blessing in our lives is because we fail to ask for it: "You do not have because you do not ask" (James 4:2).

Don decided it was time to start doing some serious asking. He recalled a period in his life when he had faithfully kept a prayer journal, recording his various requests and God's answers to those requests. That was such an exciting time in his life—seeing God answer his prayers in such specific ways. Don couldn't recall when or why he quit keeping his prayer journal, but now he was ready to begin again.

He accepted the book's challenge and boldly asked God to bless him in three very specific ways—all of which would certainly bring glory to God. First, he prayed that his nineteen-year-old daughter would break up with her boyfriend who was not a Christian and was having an adverse effect on her spiritual life. Second, Don asked God to grant him a promotion in his company. Sure, there was a "selfish" component to this prayer—he and his wife could certainly use the extra income. But the promotion would also afford Don the opportunity to exert a greater influence for Christ in his company. Finally, Don prayed that God would heal his brother, who recently had been diagnosed with pancreatic cancer. Such a miraculous healing would be an undeniable testimony to the power of God.

For the next three months, Don faithfully spent the first fifteen minutes of every morning praying for these requests. By the end of those three months, the following events had transpired:

- Don's daughter announced her engagement to her boyfriend;
- due to an economic slowdown, Don's company eliminated the position he was seeking; and
- Don's brother died.

Now Don remembered why he had quit praying.

THE "PRAYER FADE" PHENOMENON

One writer calls it the "prayer fade." You may not be familiar with the term, but you no doubt have experienced the reality behind the phrase. A book, a seminar, a sermon, or a moment of desperation convinces you that the missing ingredient in your relationship with God is a consistent prayer life. You are reminded that all of the Bible's great men and women of faith had one thing in common: They were devoted to prayer. Even Jesus Christ, the Son of God, would arise in the early morning before it was light to devote hours to communicating with His heavenly Father. If prayer was a necessity for Jesus Himself, we are told, how much more necessary is it for us?

Convinced that you need to be more devoted to prayer, you develop a disciplined plan for praying...and it lasts a few days, weeks, or months (you fill in the blank) until you give up, disgusted with your lack of discipline and disappointed with God's lack of answers. One Christian describes his own "prayer fade" this way:

When I was a new believer, the thought of talking with the God of the universe, the thought of him listening to me, responding to my cares and concerns, was so overwhelming I could barely take it in. I prayed all the time when I first discovered I could. I prayed when I got up. I prayed on my way to work. I prayed when I sat at my desk. I prayed at lunch. I prayed with my kids at dinner. I prayed with my

kids when I put them to bed…. It brought me such joy.
God was answering my prayers. My life was changing, and
I could see others' lives changing.

Then I don't know what happened. The whole deal just
cooled off. I don't pray much any more.[1]

Sound familiar? We've all been there, haven't we? And yet, as
you search the Scriptures, it is obvious that prayer is another conduit through which the Holy Spirit's power is released in our lives.

- It was through prayer that the fire from heaven fell and
  consumed the animal sacrifices on Mount Carmel.
- It was through prayer that Jesus miraculously fed more
  than five thousand people with five loaves and two fish.
- It was through prayer that the power of God filled the
  disciples on the Day of Pentecost.
- It was through prayer that Peter was supernaturally
  released from prison.

And the list goes on. Recently I saw the power of prayer
demonstrated in our church. For a year we have been wrestling
with a decision about relocating our church as we make plans for
a new worship center. Our leaders decided to put out a "fleece"
that was based on sound logic. For us to remain at our present loca-
tion, we needed permission from the city to close a street separat-
ing our main facility from the site of the new sanctuary. This
would enable us to connect the new worship center with our exist-
ing structure. Our initial appeal to the city failed. We were told
that we could appeal if we wanted to, but most likely they would
stand by their decision.

Early one Wednesday morning last spring, I met with about
fifty of my Pastor's Prayer Partners to discuss various prayer concerns, including the closing of the street. Suddenly I felt one of
those inner promptings I wrote about earlier.

"Instead of just talking about this problem, why don't we walk down to the sanctuary and pray about it?" I proposed.

So all fifty of us marched down to the sanctuary, knelt at the altar, and spent about thirty minutes on our knees discussing the situation with God. At 4:30 that afternoon, the city manager called me and said, "I would like to talk with you about the possibility of closing the street." Within a month all of the details were worked out, and the street was ours.

Coincidence? I don't think so.

I imagine you could also relate some examples of extraordinary miracles that were the direct result of prayer. So then, why don't we pray more? Some might say that it is the busyness of life that keeps us from praying. And yet, as packed as most of our schedules are, we find a way to make time for eating, recreation, and other activities we deem vital.

Richard Foster has one answer for the prayerlessness that I think characterizes so many of us:

> It is the notion—almost universal among us modern high achievers—that we have to have everything "just right" in order to pray. That is, before we can really pray, our lives need some fine tuning, or we need to know more about how to pray, or we need to study the philosophical questions surrounding prayer, or we need to have a better grasp of the great traditions of prayer. And on it goes…. Our problem is that we assume prayer is something we master the way we master algebra or auto mechanics.[2]

So right away I want to confide two reassuring secrets that should relieve much of the anxiety and apprehension you may have about prayer. Ready?

SECRET NO. 1: YOU WILL ALWAYS
STRUGGLE WITH PRAYER

I don't use the word *struggle* lightly. The apostle Paul used the word in Romans 15:30 when he asked the Christians in Rome to "strive together with me in your prayers." The root word translated *strive* is *agonizomai*. (Sounds painful, doesn't it?) The word was used to describe the struggle experienced by a wrestler in an athletic contest.

Make no mistake about it, prayer is hard work. Why?

When we pray, we are, first of all, wrestling with an enemy who is bent on our destruction. The last thing Satan wants is for us to experience more of God's power and blessing. Paul declared the reality of that struggle when he wrote,

> For our struggle is not against flesh and blood, but against
> the rulers, against the powers, against the world forces of
> this darkness, against the spiritual forces of wickedness in
> the heavenly places. (Ephesians 6:12)

And at times, prayer is also a struggle with God. Both Jacob in the Old Testament and Jesus in the New Testament found themselves wrestling with God over submission to His will for their lives. Luke tells us that Jesus struggled in prayer to the point that "His sweat became like drops of blood, falling down upon the ground" (Luke 22:44). Frankly, it sometimes requires a lot of blood, sweat, and tears to resolve the not-my-will-but-Thy-will issue.

But the biggest struggle we face in prayer is with ourselves. Getting up in the morning and gaining blanket victory will always be hard. Declining that extra episode of our favorite sitcom, some late-breaking news on CNN, or another chapter in our new novel in favor of moments of solitude with God will always be a struggle. So will concentrating on conversation with God instead of mentally reviewing our to-do list or rehearsing an argument we've just had or are about to have.

The good news is that God understands our weaknesses. "He… knows our frame; He is mindful that we are but dust," says the psalmist (103:14). Yet sometimes we have more difficulty than God does in accepting our limitations. Brother Lawrence once wrote,

> For many years I was bothered by the thought I was a failure at prayer. Then one day I realized that I would always be a failure at prayer; and I've gotten along much better ever since.[3]

SECRET NO. 2: YOU DON'T HAVE TO BE GOOD AT PRAYER TO BE EFFECTIVE IN PRAYER

How do I know that? Consider just a few examples of what some would consider "ineffective" prayer by today's standards.

- Elijah's prayer on Mount Carmel lacked length (only sixty-three words in the NASB English text), yet God miraculously consumed the animal sacrifices.
- Peter's prayer lacked both length and depth (what could be more selfish than praying "Lord, save me"), yet Jesus lifted him up out of the boiling sea.
- The Christians praying for Peter's release from prison lacked faith (Peter had an easier time getting *out of* prison than *into* the homes of the Christians who had gathered to pray for him), yet God supernaturally delivered their leader.

In commenting on that story found in Acts 12, Greg Laurie wrote:

> This passage, among others, debunks the popular teaching among some that says our faith makes all the difference in

prayer and that faith is some kind of active force that we have to harness and use. We are told that we have to say the right thing. We have to give a "positive confession." We have to speak the miracle into existence. According to this theology, almost everything about prayer revolves around the quality of our faith. It certainly was a good thing for Peter that this isn't true![4]

Fortunately, God does not require a Ph.D. in intercessory prayer before we can approach Him with our requests and appropriate His power in our lives. However, I do believe there are at least four common questions we need to answer before we will ever consistently experience more of God's power through prayer.

The *Power* of Prayer: "Why Pray If God Is Going to Do What He Wants Anyway?"

That's a question one of our members asked me recently while I was making my way down the hallway to—of all places—prayer meeting. (Maybe he was looking for a theological excuse to skip the service in favor of a new episode of *The West Wing*.) It's a good question, you will have to admit. Does prayer actually change God's plan, or does it simply change my ability to accept God's plan? I agree with the late James Montgomery Boice, who pointed out that Christians tend to go to one of two extremes in answering this question.

Some say that God's power is limited by our willingness to pray. In his book *Why Pray?* William Evans observed:

> Prayer does not change God's purposes and plans; but it releases them and permits God to do in, for, and through us all which his infinite love and wisdom want to do, but which because of lack of prayer he has not been able to do.

We should not think that God can do whatever he wants to do without our aid. He cannot.[5]

Whoa, there! God "cannot do" whatever He wishes? Whatever happened to the God "who is able to do far more abundantly beyond all that we ask or think" (Ephesians 3:20)? To limit God's power by our prayers is to strip God of His sovereignty—something we should not, and thankfully, *cannot* do.

At the other extreme are those who correctly proclaim the sovereignty of God but incorrectly conclude that prayer is unnecessary because God's plan will ultimately be accomplished regardless of our actions. These are the same people who correctly teach "election" (that God has determined who will be saved) but eliminate the need for evangelism, concluding that "God will save whom He is going to save without any help from me."

I like how one theologian countered, "God not only ordains the end result, but He also ordains the means by which He will accomplish that result." For example, I might say to my girls on Saturday morning, "I want the playroom to be cleaned up today." I have decreed what I want to happen, and it *will* happen. But I have also ordained the means by which the task will be accomplished: my daughters' efforts.

Yes, God has determined who will be saved, but He has also determined the means by which they will be saved: the evangelistic efforts of Christians. "So faith comes from hearing, and hearing by the word of Christ" (Romans 10:17).

In the same way, God has a plan that governs the entire universe as well as our individual lives: "'For I know the plans that I have for you,' declares the LORD, 'plans for welfare and not for calamity to give you a future and a hope'" (Jeremiah 29:11).

And God has determined that prayer is the means by which He pours those blessings into our lives.

The same apostle Paul who believed strongly in the sovereignty of God—"So then it does not depend on the man who wills or the man who runs, but on God who has mercy" (Romans 9:16)—also strongly believed in the power of prayer—"Now I urge you, brethren, by our Lord Jesus Christ and by the love of the Spirit, to strive together with me in your prayers to God for me" (Romans 15:30). Yes, prayer changes me, but in some inexplicable way it changes my situation as well.

THE *PATTERN* FOR PRAYER: "WHAT SORT OF THINGS SHOULD I PRAY FOR?"

Is it wrong to pray for a promotion, a bigger salary, or a larger home? Is it more spiritual to pray, "Lord, heal me from this disease," or to pray, "Lord, Your will be done?"

Again, Christians go to one of two extremes in answering these questions. Some view heaven as a divine vending machine and prayer as the coinage by which we receive all of the goodies our little hearts can imagine.

Others, understandably repulsed by that view of intercession, go to the opposite extreme, encouraging fellow believers to abstain from "selfish" requests for money, happiness, or healing and instead focus solely on God's glory. We are told that the most immature kind of prayer is "me-centered praying." When we grow in spiritual maturity, we are told, we move from "me-centered" praying to "other-centered" praying, placing other people's needs above our own. But the highest level of prayer is "God-centered" praying in which we refuse to mention our (or other people's) needs in deference to the furtherance of God's kingdom.

Fortunately, Jesus provides a balanced view of prayer that includes requests for ourselves, for others, and for God's glory. The model prayer, recorded in Matthew 6, was the result of the disciples' request, "Lord, teach us to pray" (Luke 11:1) By observing the Master, the disciples had concluded that the secret to Jesus' supernatural power was His devotion to prayer. For Jesus, prayer was not a nicety, but a necessity. And so the disciples asked Jesus for some simple instruction about how to pray so that they might also experience God's supernatural working in their lives.

Jesus responded by giving the disciples (and us) a pattern to follow—five essential components of effective prayer.

PRAISE OF GOD'S NAME

"Our Father who is in heaven, hallowed be Your name." Many of us have recited this phrase for years without any understanding of what it really means. There are two key words in this phrase: *name* and *hallowed*.

A person's name represents his entire being. When someone says your name to a person who knows you, your name evokes a picture in that other person's mind. He thinks about your appearance, your voice, and your personality. Your name represents who you are. In the same way, when Jesus speaks of God's name, He is referring to God's entire being.

The word *hallowed* comes from a word that means "holy." The word *holy* gets thrown around a lot in church circles without any comprehension of its true meaning. *Holy* means "separate" or "different." Thus, when we put the words *name* and *hallowed* together, we gain a better understanding of the pattern Jesus is modeling for us: Before we start rushing at God with all of our requests and concerns—there will be plenty of time for that—we are to begin our prayer by acknowledging how different God is from anyone or anything here on earth.

"God, thank You for Your faithfulness to me, even when I have been unfaithful to You."

"God, I praise You for loving me when I deserved nothing but Your judgment."

"God, I recognize that You are righteous and have no tolerance for sin."

"God, I acknowledge that You are wiser than I am and have a plan for my life that is beyond my comprehension."

PRIORITY OF GOD'S PURPOSE

When Jesus instructed us to pray, "Your kingdom come. Your will be done, on earth as it is in heaven," He was instructing us to pray for the *future return* of Christ ("Your kingdom come") but also for the *present rule* of Christ ("Your will be done, on earth").

Since, as the late Speaker of the House, Tip O'Neill, used to say, "All politics are local," let's apply that prayer request to our personal lives. In praying for God's will to be done, we are subjugating our desires and plans to God's desires and plans for us. When we pray, "Your will be done," we are saying to God…

- *"I will accept Your providential will."* God's providential will is that secret plan that governs all that happens in the universe as well as all that happens in our lives. Usually, God's providential will is best seen in the rearview mirror. Rarely does He allow us to know beforehand what events are going to transpire. But we accept God's providential will when we say, "God, even though I don't understand what is happening in my life, I am still trusting in You. Even though I can't see Your hand, I am trusting Your heart."
- *"I will obey Your preceptive will."* God's preceptive will involves God's desires for our lives that are clearly spelled out in the Bible. Frankly, most of us struggle more with the part of God's will that we already know than with the part we do not know. For example, can you identify one thing in your life that you know God wants you to start

doing or stop doing? I imagine several things immediately come to your mind. When we pray, "Your will be done, on earth as it is in heaven" we are saying, "God, right now I am going to start obeying You just as the angels in heaven obey You."

PROVISION FOR OUR NEEDS

Although God's will should be the primary focus of our prayers, it does not have to be the exclusive focus of our prayers. The remainder of Jesus' model prayer deals with the very real needs we have, needs that Jesus says we should boldly ask God to meet.

For example, we have physical needs, as evidenced by the phrase, "Give us this day our daily bread." I think Jesus has more in mind here than a loaf of Wonder Bread. The term *bread* in Scripture is used to refer to food in general. Jesus is encouraging us to ask God to provide our basic needs, which include food, shelter, clothing, transportation, and even the job by which we can earn the funds to pay for these necessities. After all, even our ability to earn a living to provide for these needs comes from God: "But you shall remember the LORD your God, for it is He who is giving you power to make wealth" (Deuteronomy 8:18).

As one writer points out, however, Jesus did not instruct us to pray, "Give us this day our daily steak and lobster." In Philippians 4:19, Paul wrote, "And my God will supply all your *needs,*" not "My God will satisfy all your *greeds.*"

PARDON FOR OUR SINS

Our prayers should also include a plea for God's forgiveness for our sins. "And forgive us our debts, as we also have forgiven our debtors."

You might wonder, If I am a Christian and God has already forgiven me of my sins, why do I need to ask for God's forgiveness again? Here it is helpful to remember that there is a difference between God's judicial forgiveness and God's parental forgiveness. When I become a Christian, God declares me "not guilty" of all of my transgressions—past, present, and future—in the court of heaven. That is judicial forgiveness. But such forgiveness does not exempt me from experiencing God's parental disapproval and disappointment. Although my disobedience does not remove me from God's family, it does disrupt my relationship with my heavenly Father. Every parent reading these words knows what it is like to feel estranged from a beloved child because of the child's disobedience, disrespect, or disinterest in you.

To reestablish our broken relationship with God, Jesus says all we must do is ask—genuinely ask—for God's forgiveness. I should add that such a request is more than a mere cataloguing of our mistakes. I remember hearing all sorts of erroneous teaching as a teenager about the Christian life, including the idea that "to confess your sins" means simply to "acknowledge your sin" to God. No tears or remorse are necessary, just a mutual agreement with God that you've messed up.

Compare that kind of cool, unemotional "repentance" with Paul's emotion-packed cry of "Wretched man that I am!" (Romans 7:24) or with David's explanation of the kind of repentance that moves the heart of God: "The sacrifices of God are a broken spirit; a broken and a contrite heart, O God, You will not despise" (Psalm 51:17). True confession involves an inner brokenness because of our sins.

Confession is also more than expressing heartfelt disappointment for our mistakes. Inherent in genuine repentance is a promise to turn away from the sins we confess to God. Lewis Smedes asks:

> Why should you expect anyone to take your confession
> seriously unless you promise that you do not intend again
> to foul your relationship with still more of the same unfair

pain? You can give no guarantee; the best of us go back on promises. But anyone who has been hurt should expect a sincere intention, at least…. The level of our promise [to do better] helps us to know whether we are actually repenting or just attempting damage control.[6]

PROTECTION FROM EVIL

Finally, Jesus urges us to ask God for deliverance from difficult situations. "And do not lead us into temptation, but deliver us from evil." The word translated *temptation* means "a difficult situation."

It might sound strange to ask God to exempt us from trials in life. After all, don't difficult situations strengthen our faith? Well, sometimes, but not always. For every Christian who has been drawn closer to God through illness, financial hardship, or the death of a loved one, there are others who have turned away from God because of those same difficulties. In fact, I imagine you could name a few. Trials in life are like tests in school—they can result in either success or failure.

That's why Jesus says there is nothing wrong with asking God to exempt you from tests. In fact, David prayed that way. In Psalm 22, he pleaded with God to

Deliver my soul from the sword, my only life from the power of the dog. Save me from the lion's mouth; from the horns of the wild oxen You answer me. (verses 20-21)

One recent Sunday I was explaining to our congregation that David was praying for protection from common sources of danger in his day: warfare, animal attacks, and accidents. "If David were praying this prayer today, he might say, 'Lord deliver me from muggers, from drive-by shootings, or from those SUVs whirring by me on the freeway.'" After the first service I received a note from one of our members that I read to the congregation in the next service (I promise I'm not making this up): *Dear Pastor, I couldn't agree with you more. I can't stand those SOBs that whiz by me on the freeway!*

But in the event that God allows such a trial in my life, I am to ask Him to bring me safely through that trial. "Lord, I don't understand why this is happening, but I still believe You are in control. Keep me from turning away from You, and use this difficulty to make me more like Christ."[7]

I don't think that Jesus ever intended this model prayer to be an exhaustive list of everything we should pray for, although I have a hard time thinking of anything that would not fit into one of these five broad categories. The short, simple answer to the question "What sort of things should I pray about?" is "Anything that you're concerned about."

THE *PROBLEM* OF PRAYER: "WHY DOESN'T GOD ANSWER MY PRAYERS?"

Name one unanswered prayer request in your life. It's amazing, isn't it, how quickly one (or two or three) come to mind?

From our earliest days of praying, we learned the hard truth that God does not answer all of our prayers, whether they are childhood requests for a specific toy, adolescent pleadings for a specific boyfriend or girlfriend, or adult pleas for healing for ourselves or for a loved one. Rack up enough noes in your prayer life, and you may conclude that either (a) "I'm not very good at this praying stuff," or (b) "God does not listen or care—or maybe He doesn't even exist." Either way, you may be tempted to drift into the "prayer fade" we described earlier.

Why does God sometimes say no to our prayers? As I look through the Scriptures, at least three answers jump off the pages.

WRONG ACTIONS

Often, it is our disobedience to God that keeps Him from answering our requests. God said to the Israelites, "Your iniquities have made a separation between you and your God, and your sins have hidden His face from you so that He does not hear" (Isaiah 59:2). God was not speaking to the heathen who needed His *judicial* forgiveness, but to His own children who needed His *parental* forgiveness. Their continuing sin prevented God from hearing and answering their prayers.

When the late author and pastor Norman Vincent Peale was a small boy, he found a cigar and decided to experiment with the forbidden. When Peale saw his father approaching, he attempted to hide the cigar and distract his dad by pointing to a sign advertising a circus that was coming to town. "Dad, do you think we could go to the circus together?" Peale's father replied, "Son, I've learned never to petition your father when you're holding smoldering disobedience in your hand." Good advice for all of us to consider before we petition our Father!

WRONG MOTIVES

James gave two simple explanations for the lack of God's supernatural blessing in our lives. One is obvious: "You do not have because you do not ask" (James 4:2). Here is a simple but often overlooked truth: *Asking* for God's blessings is a prerequisite for *receiving* God's blessings.

I was recently in a small group of pastors in which my friend Adrian Rogers related this story. While Dr. Rogers was attending Bible college in Florida, he was invited to preach at a small church one Sunday. The church did not have enough money to pay him an honorarium, so the head deacon gave him a large burlap sack filled with oranges—more oranges than he could eat in a year!

Dr. Rogers drove back to his little second-story apartment,

lugged that heavy bag of oranges up the stairs, and stored them in a closet. A few days later while he was studying, Dr. Rogers looked out his window and saw a little boy from next door climbing over the fence. The boy stood on top of the fence and was attempting to steal an orange from the orange tree in Dr. Rogers's backyard. Dr. Rogers watched with fascination as the boy looked both ways to make sure no one was watching as he placed the purloined orange in the pocket of his overalls. What the little boy didn't know was that it was a sour orange. A sour orange resembles a regular orange in every way—until you put it into your mouth.

Dr. Rogers chuckled to himself as he imagined that boy reaching into his overalls for the stolen orange, peeling it, taking a big bite, and receiving what he so richly deserved. Then Dr. Rogers said to us, "You know, had that boy simply walked up our stairs, knocked on the door, and asked, I would have given him an orange. In fact, I would have gone to the closet and given him more oranges than he could have ever dreamed of. He had not because he asked not."

As someone once said, "The devil cannot keep God from answering, but he *can* keep us from asking."

If there is going to be any regret in heaven, I believe it will occur when we see all the indescribable blessings God had planned to give us if only we had exercised the faith to ask. I personally believe one reason there is so much sickness among Christians today is because of their failure to ask God for supernatural healing. In the next chapter, James tells us that if anyone is sick, he should call on the elders of the church, "and they are to pray over him, anointing him with oil in the name of the Lord" (5:14). There are a variety of opinions concerning the significance of the oil in this passage, but the main verb used here is *pray.* When we are seriously ill, we should have godly leaders pray for us. In our church, we regularly have our leaders pray over those with life-threatening illnesses. Sometimes at the end of the service, I call for all who are sick to come to the altar so that we might pray over them. Yes, I understand that it is not always God's will to heal everyone who is sick. But *sometimes* it is! God is more than willing to heal many who are sick today if only we have the faith to ask. We have not because we ask not.

Then James gives us a second explanation for unanswered prayer: "You ask and do not receive, because you ask with wrong motives, so that you may spend it on your pleasures" (4:3). Admittedly, identifying and evaluating our motives can be tricky, since our own hearts are "deceitful" and "desperately wicked," as the prophet Jeremiah pointed out (KJV). Furthermore, how does one define "wrong motives"? When Jesus invites us to pray for food and protection, isn't He encouraging "selfish" motives? Frankly, it is impossible to pray with completely pure motives—or even define them for that matter! However, as Richard Foster reminds us, that should not keep us from praying:

> The truth of the matter is, we all come to prayer with a
> tangled mass of motives—altruistic *and* selfish, merciful
> *and* hateful, loving *and* bitter. Frankly, this side of eternity
> we will *never* unravel the good from the bad, the pure from
> the impure. But what I have come to see is that God is big
> enough to receive us with all our mixture. We do not have
> to be bright, or pure, or filled with faith, or anything. That
> is what grace means, and not only are we saved by grace, we
> live by it as well. And we pray by it.[8]

Instead of engaging in endless introspection, I believe James is asking us to examine the major motivation that drives our life. Is it self-centered or God-centered? Are we striving to build our own kingdoms or God's kingdom? Are we determined to get our way, or are we willing to submit to God's desires for our life? Our answers to those macroquestions will in large part determine the degree of success we experience in prayer.

Wrong Requests

A minister friend asked me this question over lunch today: "Robert, what is the 'prayer of faith' described in the Bible? Do I have to believe that God is going to answer my prayer request before He will do so?"

My friend went on to tell me that he had been asked to pray for healing for a terminally ill patient. How much faith did he need to have that the man would be healed in order for God to answer his request? If God did not want to heal that person, was my friend praying in vain? And if he prayed, "God, Your will be done," wasn't that the ultimate cop-out?

We all probably would agree that faith is an important ingredient to successful prayer. The Bible tells us that without faith it is impossible to please God (see Hebrews 11:6). But what exactly does it mean to pray with faith? Is faith just a spiritualized synonym for the positive-thinking mantra, "Whatever the mind can conceive and believe, it can achieve"?

First, let's understand that God has never promised to answer our every request, regardless of the amount of faith we exercise. Any promise in the Bible of unconditional answers to prayer still must fall within the boundary of God's perfect will. The apostle John wrote: "This is the confidence which we have before Him, that, if we ask anything *according to His will,* He hears us" (1 John 5:14).

This protective hedge around our lives called "God's will" is not meant to keep good things *out* of our lives, but to keep evil things from entering *into* our lives. For example, how would you respond if your nine-year-old child were to request a car in order to drive himself to school each day? Your child might believe that you have the financial means to purchase the car. He might even have the right motive in asking for the car—to save you from being a taxicab service. But no matter how pure his motives or how much "faith" he has conjured up that he will receive the automobile, you would say no to that request out of concern for his safety (as well as the safety of those in your neighborhood).

I don't know about you, but I shudder when I look back at some of my previous prayer requests. How grateful I am that God loved me enough to say no. Instead of discouraging us, this conditional nature of prayer should encourage us to pray even more. Why? Because the very *best* gifts we could ever hope for are found within the boundaries of God's perfect and loving will.

Second, as we attempt to define faith as it relates to prayer, we must acknowledge that we rarely can know God's will ahead of time. Certainly, there are some things we should never ask for because they violate clear teaching of Scripture. But how do we know whether God wants us to have that promotion, receive that healing, or marry that individual?

We *can't* know. In most cases God's will is best seen in retrospect. Such a realization led Paul to write, "For we do not know how to pray as we should…" (Romans 8:26). Therefore, we cannot define "faith" in terms of how strongly we believe God will answer our request. Many times we can't even know if our request is within the boundaries of God's will.

Yet in spite of our natural limitations in knowing how to pray, we can still present our requests and then rest in God's answers. That is the essence of true faith in prayer: *boldly asking* God, but *quietly trusting* Him to do what is best.

Here's something that might be an encouragement to you. Do you realize that the two greatest figures in the New Testament had to wrestle with the problem of unanswered prayer? Jesus prayed to be spared the experience of the Cross, but God said no. Paul prayed for physical healing for himself and others, and God said no.

Why did God refuse to answer Jesus' and Paul's requests? Did either of these men lack faith? Were their unanswered prayers the result of unconfessed sin in their lives? Such explanations border on the ludicrous, if not blasphemous.

God said no because He had a better plan, and Jesus and Paul willingly submitted to that plan. The object of their faith was not their desire, but their God! Far from being a spiritual cop-out, their willingness to subjugate their desires to the desire of God demonstrates the essence of true faith: trusting in the goodness and the wisdom of God.

Several months ago I visited one of our members who was dying of cancer. This woman had grown up in the theological tradition that physical healing is always God's will, that a lack of healing is the result of a lack of faith. As we sat in her front room and planned her funeral service, she smiled and said, "Robert, the most liberating truth I have discovered is that I can trust God with everything in my life, including my illness. If God wants me to be healed and stay here longer, that's fine. If God wants to take me on to heaven, that's fine too. Either way I win."

THE *PRACTICE* OF PRAYER: "HOW CAN I BECOME A BETTER PRAY-ER?"

Even though you might be a victim of "prayer fade," you now may be convinced that prayer is the channel through which you can experience more of God's supernatural power in your life. You may want to rededicate yourself to making prayer a central part of your life again. Which leads us to question, "How can I become a better pray-er?"

To attempt to cover such a question in the few remaining pages of this chapter would be ridiculous. Indeed, a number of wonderful books about prayer answer that question more completely. But to get you started in your new commitment, allow me to suggest some practical, simple practices that have been beneficial to me and, hopefully, will assist you in your quest for "more" in your relationship with God.

START SMALL

Don't fall into the trap of thinking that unless you have an hour or two to devote to prayer every day, you cannot pray effectively. While longer periods of prayer are always desirable, they are not always possible, especially when you are just beginning to establish the practice of prayer.

With that said, common sense should tell us that there are three times during each day in which *everyone* can pray, effectively mooting the "too little time" excuse.

When You Get Up...

Before your feet touch the floor in the morning, take a moment or two and talk to your heavenly Father. Offer a prayer of gratitude such as: "God, thank You for the gift of life. Thank You for protecting me through the night." Ask God for protection for yourself and your family: "Lord, keep me and my family safe today from evil and from adversity (like those SUVs!)." Submit your plans to God: "Father, You know my plans for the day, but please make me sensitive to those opportunities I have to glorify You."

C. S. Lewis offered excellent advice for our waking moments: "The moment you wake up each morning...(all) your wishes and hopes for the day rush at you like wild animals. And the first job of each morning consists in shoving them all back; in listening to that other voice, taking that other point of view, letting that other, larger, stronger, quieter life come flowing in."

As You Go Through the Day...

Max Lucado assures us that we do not have to wait for the perfect time to pray. Instead, he advises:

> Imagine considering every moment as a potential time of
> communion with God. By the time your life is over, you will
> have spent six months at stoplights, eight months opening
> junk mail, a year and a half looking for lost stuff (double that
> number in my case), and a whopping five years standing in
> various lines. Why don't you give these moments to God? By
> giving God your whispering thoughts, the common becomes
> the uncommon. Simple phrases such as "Thank you,
> Father," "Be sovereign in this hour, O Lord," "You are my
> resting place, Jesus," can turn a commute into a pilgrimage.
> You needn't leave your office or kneel in your kitchen. Just
> pray where you are. Let the kitchen become a cathedral or
> the classroom a chapel. Give God your whispering thoughts.[9]

Those kinds of practical suggestions illustrate what Paul meant by "redeeming the time."

Before You Go to Sleep...

Before you drift off to sleep, talk with God about your day. Review the high points as well as the disappointments. Tell Him what you are worried about. As the late Mary Crowley used to say, "I let God worry about my problems while I'm asleep, since He's going to be up all night anyway."

Thomas Kelly described the benefits of beginning and ending every day in prayer:

> Let inward prayer be your last act before you fall asleep and
> the first act when you awake. And in time you will find as

did Brother Lawrence, that those who have the gale of the
Holy Spirit go forward even in their sleep.[10]

WRITE OUT OR VOCALIZE YOUR PRAYERS

I used to be really annoyed by people who would read their
prayers, especially during a public worship service. For example,
when the time came for the obligatory offertory prayer, the minister would call on Deacon Smith to ask God's blessing on the col-
lection. As soon as every eye was closed and the coast was clear,
Deacon Smith would pull from his coat pocket a piece of paper on
which he had written his prayer. *What's wrong with this guy that he
can't pray for a couple of minutes without reading?* I wondered. (Yes,
I had my eyes open—call it pastoral privilege.)

Now I have come to appreciate the value of writing out my
prayers on a yellow legal pad or on my computer during my time
alone with God. I don't know about you, but I have difficulty concentrating when I'm praying (a friend says I am a poster child for
ADD). Just a few sentences into my prayer I'll find myself reviewing my to-do list or rehearsing a conversation I'm about to have or
have already had. Before long I find myself uttering spiritual banal-
ities like "Bless so and so" or "Lead, guide, and direct..." that bore
me and, I'm sure, bore God.

Writing out my prayers helps me stay focused on my conversation with God. If you find it awkward to write out your prayers,
you will find that simply vocalizing your prayers, rather than just
imagining them, will also help keep your mind from wandering.

BE HONEST WITH GOD (HE CAN HANDLE IT!)

C. S. Lewis offered some wise counsel about the content of our
prayers: "Lay before Him what is in us, not what ought to be in
us." Is there something you desire, but you are unsure whether you
should ask? Go ahead and ask—and trust God with the answer.

Are you angry with another person? You can tell God about it. No matter how hot you are, you are probably not as incensed as the psalmist who prayed that the babies of his enemies would be smashed against the rocks (see Psalm 137:9). Are you disappointed with God because of His action or inaction? His shoulders are broad enough and His love is wide enough to handle your frustration.

In the end, prayer is neither a theological formula nor a religious ritual. Instead, prayer is an intimate conversation with the Creator of the Universe who loves us and is vitally concerned with every part of our lives. As John Bunyan wrote, "Prayer is a sincere, sensible, affectionate pouring out of the heart or soul to God, through Christ." But beyond conversation, prayer is a channel through which the power of God is ignited in our lives.

Seven

UP WITH WORSHIP!

Finding and Thriving in a Spirit-Powered Church

Rick and Sharon Ballew hated to move for a number of reasons. Uprooting their three children—one in elementary school and two in high school—was unsettling enough. The soft real estate environment would no doubt make selling their recently remodeled home difficult. And the uncertainty of a new job carried its own kind of stress.

But the primary reason the Ballews regretted moving was their church. Rick and Sharon had met each other fifteen years earlier in the singles' group at Stonecreek Community Church. All three of their children had become Christians in large part because of the excellent children's and youth ministries at Stonecreek. Pastor Ted Davis was an excellent Bible teacher who could always be counted on to come through with a message that was both informative and inspirational. Rick and Sharon had been involved in the same small-group fellowship for the past ten years. The Ballews felt closer to the other five couples in their group than they did to some of their own family. Over the years they had prayed for one another's children, cried together over the unexpected tragedies that a decade brings, and taken care of one another's needs ranging from financial assistance to all-night hospital vigils.

How could Rick and Sharon ever hope to find another church like Stonecreek? Nevertheless, after arriving in their new community and taking a few Sundays off to unpack and reacclimate, the Ballews were ready to begin their hunt for a new church. They decided to begin with a church right around the corner from their home.

Gardendale Bible Church advertised itself as nondenominational, much like their previous church. But that is where the similarity ended. Unlike the contemporary worship services at Stonecreek, Gardendale's congregational singing consisted of songs from a hymnal.

Rick whispered to Sharon, "I didn't know they still *made* hymnals."

After the robed choir sang an arrangement of "A Mighty Fortress Is Our God," the pastor preached a forty-five-minute message from Ezekiel 40 concerning the millennial temple, complete with an outline that actually showed the dimensions of the future temple. The sermon was high on scriptural content, but low on application. What really surprised the Ballews, however, was the fact that not one individual had spoken to them during their one-and-a-half-hour visit to the church. Surely there was something better.

The next week the Ballews were invited by their new next-door neighbor to attend First Baptist Church. Since neither Rick nor Sharon had ever been part of a denomination, they were reluctant. The thought of an *even more* traditional service than the one they had just attended made them dread Sunday. However, they were surprised at how different the service was from what they had anticipated. They could not get from the car to the sanctuary without several people greeting them. They were also amazed to see that there were no hymnals in the church and no choir. Instead, a praise team of twelve energetic singers led the congregation in a seamless flow of music. For those unfamiliar with the songs, words were conveniently projected on a large screen at the front of the sanctuary.

"This is more like it!" Sharon whispered to Rick.

Finally, it was time for the sermon. The pastor walked up from the congregation wearing an open-collar shirt and sat on a stool in the middle of the stage. Instead of "preaching," he employed a conversational style that disarmed the audience. After citing some statistics about the high degree of stress people were experiencing, he said, "Today I want to share with you four 'stress-busters.'" The pastor spent the next twenty minutes sharing some extremely practical tips for dealing with pressure, but he never once opened a Bible or even made more than a passing reference to Scripture. Rick and Sharon left the service perplexed. While the music was definitely appealing to them, they felt that the message was one that could have been delivered just as easily at a Rotary Club meeting as in a church.

The hunt continued.

The next week the Ballews accepted an invitation from a coworker to attend his church. New Hope Cathedral was different from any church the Ballews had ever experienced. The music portion of the service was even more lively than First Baptist's and lasted considerably longer. During one set of songs, the praise team actually danced on the stage and encouraged the congregation to fill the aisles "dancing unto the Lord." Unlike the stereotypical charismatic services the Ballews had heard about or imagined, everything in the service—even the dancing—was done decently and in order. There was no rolling in the aisles or handling of serpents. In the middle of the song service, the worship leader invited those who desired emotional or physical healing to come to the altar for prayer. The Ballews were astonished when it seemed that several hundred went forward. A group of associate pastors and lay leaders stood at the front and, just as James 5 instructed, anointed those who requested prayer with oil. Then the pastor prayed over the people for at least five minutes.

After the people returned to their seats, the pastor then preached the best message the Ballews had heard in the last several weeks. The message was titled "The Greatest Promise in the Bible" and was based on Romans 8:28: "And we know that God causes all things to work together for good to those who love God, to those who are called according to His purpose." The sermon was both biblical and practical, but it only confounded the Ballews' church decision even more. They loved the message and found parts of the music service inspiring. However, they just weren't sure they felt comfortable with the dancing and healing portion of the service.

One day at her daughter's soccer practice, Sharon was casually sharing with one of the other moms the difficulty her family was having in finding a church home. "I know what you mean," the other mom sighed. "That's why we gave up and decided to start our own." Sharon asked what she meant, and Susie explained that every Thursday evening eight couples met together for a potluck meal, a time of fellowship and prayer, and a Bible study, which they took turns leading. "We don't have a pastor or elders or any complicated organization. Not even an offering!" Susie joked. "It's all very laid back, and we get more out of our time together than we ever did out of any church we ever attended."

That night after the children were asleep Rick and Sharon discussed their church shopping dilemma. They tried to answer the obvious questions:

"What is most important in a church—great music or excellent preaching?"

"Why isn't there a church that seems to have both?"

But then their discussion turned more philosophical. In fact—they laughed—their musings even bordered on the heretical.

"Is church really that important?"

"Doesn't there need to be a new model for the church that eliminates all of the hierarchy and meaningless activities that only clutter people's already-too-busy lives?"

"What is a church anyway?"

A VITAL CONNECTION

As we have attempted to answer the question, "What can I do to experience more of God's power in my life?" we have looked at two obvious, but nevertheless neglected, conduits of God's energy: the Word of God (the Bible) and conversing with God (prayer). In this chapter, we are going to discover another source of spiritual power that, to paraphrase comedian Rodney Dangerfield, "doesn't get no respect" these days: the church.

One of the major arteries through which God's spiritual energy flows into our lives is a local body of believers. Without that vital connection to other believers, we become like a limb that is severed from the body. We will quickly atrophy and eventually die.

I realize that such a statement runs counter to our culture of rugged individualism. We like to think we can maintain our own relationship with God without any interference from other people or, heaven forbid, an organization. George Gallup Jr., who regularly surveys the attitudes of Americans toward religion, discovered that 70 percent of all professing Christians in America believe that it is possible to have a vital relationship with God without attending church. Many people view the church just like any other organization: with its own hierarchy, its own political struggles, its own flaws. One person said, "Now I see the church not much differently than the government. Both are overpowering. They just build buildings and take money. The buildings, the foreign mission programs are nice, but the church has become a power broker."[1]

And yet, in spite of its flaws and potential pitfalls, the church is central to God's plan for the world in general, and to our lives in particular. How do I know that?

Consider Jesus' attitude toward the church. He does not simply tolerate the church, or view it as some necessary evil. Instead, Jesus *loves* the church. As the apostle Paul wrote:

> Husbands, love your wives, *just as Christ also loved the church* and gave Himself up for her, so that He might sanctify her, having cleansed her by the washing of water with the word, that He might present to Himself the church in all her glory, having no spot or wrinkle or any such thing; but that she would be holy and blameless. (Ephesians 5:25-27)

One word of clarification is needed here. When Paul talked about "the church," he obviously was referring to all Christians. The moment we are baptized with the Holy Spirit, as we saw in chapter 2, we become part of a mystical union called the "body of Christ" (1 Corinthians 12:27, NIV). We are spiritually joined to every other believer, as well as to Jesus Christ. Sometimes the Bible uses the word *church* in reference to all Christians everywhere, as in this passage. But the vast majority of times in the Bible the word *church* refers to a local group of Christians who have organized themselves for the purpose of accomplishing God's will. The late Francis Schaeffer defined the local church as "the Body of Christ cut down to size." Whether we are talking about the *universal church* (all Christians everywhere) or the *local church* (which is the focus of the New Testament), Paul expressed two important truths about Christ's attitude toward the church.

CHRIST CREATED THE CHURCH

I read recently about a mother who was diagnosed with cancer and told that her only hope of survival was an aggressive series of radiation treatments. A few weeks later, the woman discovered that she was also pregnant. She faced an indescribable dilemma. If she received the radiation treatments, she might live, but her baby would die. For the mother, there was no choice. She refused the treatments, gave birth to a baby girl, and died a few weeks later. She died in order that her baby might live.

Jesus not only died for us individually, but He also died for us collectively. By His death He gave birth to this spiritual organism known as the church. "Christ...loved the church and gave Himself...for her." The next time you are tempted to think that your church is taking too much of your time, energy, and money, just remember what Jesus gave in order to create this unique organism.

CHRIST SELECTED THE CHURCH

"So that He might sanctify her." As we have seen already, the word *sanctify* means "to set apart for a special purpose." God's primary purpose for our lives individually is that we become like Christ in our attitudes, actions, and affections. But what God wants for us individually, He also desires for us collectively. God has always had a special group of people to serve as His visible representatives here on earth. In the Old Testament it was the nation of Israel; in the New Testament it is the Christian church.

It is no accident that the Bible employs the term *body of Christ* to describe the church. Since Jesus has "left the building," so to speak, we are His stand-ins until He returns to earth. The closest unbelievers will ever get to seeing or hearing Jesus Christ is by watching or listening to us. That's a sobering thought, wouldn't you say?

Dorothy Sayers noted that God underwent three great humiliations in His efforts to rescue the human race. The first was the Incarnation, when He voluntarily took on the restrictions of a human body. The second was the Cross, when He suffered public execution. But the third and perhaps greatest humiliation, Sayers said, is the church: "In an awesome act of self-denial, God entrusted his reputation to ordinary people."[2]

WHY WE ALL NEED THE CHURCH

Serving as God's representatives here on earth is one reason God created and selected the church, but it's not the only reason. A few paragraphs back I claimed that it was impossible to thrive and survive spiritually apart from involvement with a local body of believers. Although you might expect such a pronouncement from a pastor, you may wonder if it is really true. *What does God do for me through the church that I cannot do for myself?*

To answer that question, let's travel back a few thousand years and see the church as God originally designed it to be. The setting is just a few days after Christ's ascension back to heaven. As He had promised, Jesus sent His disciples the gift of the Holy Spirit, who not only joined them to Christ but also to one another. They became part of a "body" of which Jesus was the "head" and they were the individual parts. What happened as a result of their connection to this new spiritual organism?

> They were continually devoting themselves to the apostles' teaching and to fellowship, to the breaking of bread and to prayer. Everyone kept feeling a sense of awe; and many wonders and signs were taking place through the apostles. And all those who had believed were together and had all things in common.… Day by day continuing with one mind in the temple, and breaking bread from house to house, they were taking their meals together with gladness and sincerity of heart, praising God and having favor with all the people. And the Lord was adding to their number day by day those who were being saved. (Acts 2:42-44,46-47)

Because of their connection to one another, these first-century believers were experiencing more of God's power than they could have ever experienced on their own. J. B. Philips wrote these words in the introduction to his paraphrase of the book of Acts:

> This surely is the Church as it was meant to be. It is vigorous and flexible, for these are the days before it ever became fat and short of breath through prosperity, or muscle-bound by overorganization. These men did not make "acts of faith," they believed; they did not "say their prayers," they really prayed. They did not hold conferences on psychosomatic medicine, they simply healed the sick. But if they were uncomplicated and naive by modern standards, we have ruefully to admit that they were open on the Godward side in a way that is almost unknown today.[3]

As I read this description of the spiritual vitality that surged through the early church, I find four benefits a church offers us that we cannot provide for ourselves. These benefits form an acrostic that spells the word WINS.

WORSHIP

I have to admit that I'm getting a little tired of hearing about "worship." It has to be at the top of the list of overused words in the latest edition of the official Christianese dictionary. We have "worship services," not church services. No longer do we have ministers of music, we have "worship leaders." Instead of meeting in a sanctuary, we assemble in the "worship center." In our denomination, seminars on "worship" have replaced seminars on building an effective Sunday-school or evangelism ministry. My wife has contemplated writing a magazine article on "The Worship of Worship."

And yet worship was definitely a priority for the early church.

Luke said that these first-century Christians devoted themselves to "praising God and having favor with all the people."

What is "worship"? Author Donald McCullough illustrated the essence of worship by recounting what he and his wife experienced upon hearing a live performance by the great tenor Luciano Pavarotti:

> The concert exceeded our expectations. We were stunned by the master's music. In aria after aria he demonstrated remarkable talent—talent, surely, that set him apart from the thousands who had come to hear him. But that set-apartness was revealed in his generous giving, his uniqueness was shown in a gracious offering of himself. He held nothing back, it seemed. Every single note was filled with boundless passion and glorious beauty.
>
> We *had* to respond: we jumped to our feet and we clapped, hooted, and whistled. We did not stop, not for a long time. Wave after wave of grateful applause was sent up to the platform, calling forth encore after encore.
>
> In the midst of this mayhem of gratitude, when my hands were beginning to ache from the pounding, I thought to myself, *This is deeply satisfying, a profound joy.* It felt right to offer praise in response to such excellence, and this sense of appropriateness created a congruence in which my little world, at least for the moment, seemed perfectly ordered.[4]

That's worship in a nutshell. It is expressing our admiration to God for who He is as well as for what He has done for us. David gave a very succinct explanation of worship when he wrote, "O magnify the LORD with me, and let us exalt His name together" (Psalm 34:3). When we put something under a magnifying glass, it causes the object to look larger. Similarly, when we magnify God's name, we are enlarging our vision of who He is.

Someone might argue, "Doesn't the magnifying glass make an object appear larger than it really is? Doesn't magnification distort reality?" Vision is a matter of perspective. For example, two pennies placed in front of your eyes have the ability to block the entire sun from your view. How is that possible, since the sun is billions of times larger than the penny? It is because the penny is closer to your eyes, even though it is infinitely smaller than the sun. In the same way, we often allow our work, relationships, financial stresses, and a thousand other "pennies" to block our vision of God and distort reality. We allow the everyday concerns of life to eclipse our view of God, and the result is that our lives are filled with unnecessary stress and unrealistic fears. Because we spend most of our time dealing with these concerns, they can seem bigger than they really are.

That is why we need a regular time each week to refocus our attention on God's love, His holiness, His faithfulness, and His purpose so that He completely fills our vision. That is the primary purpose of worship.

As I look through Scripture, I find four characteristics of authentic worship.

Genuine Worship Centers on God, Not on Us

Pastor Bob Russell offers this analogy to describe genuine worship:

> The University of Kentucky basketball team won the National Championship a couple of years ago. A few days later there was a celebration in the Rupp Arena to honor the team. The audience cheered wildly for each player when he was introduced. The fans carried banners. They painted their faces and proudly wore blue-and-white outfits. They

tried to get autographs. Not one fan walked away saying, "That event was a dud. It did nothing for me." The event was a success, not because the performance was great (they didn't play any basketball at all) or the players' speeches were inspiring (most of them weren't very good speakers), but because everyone understood why they were there. The purpose was not to please the fans but to honor the team. People walked away saying, "That was great! I hope the team understands how much we appreciate them!"

The Scriptures command us: "Ascribe to the LORD the glory due his name; worship the LORD in the splendor of his holiness" (Ps. 29:2).[5]

Genuine worship results in numerous benefits for the worshiper: exhilaration of spirit, freedom from fear, and a fresh perspective on life, just to name a few. But those benefits should never be confused with the purpose of worship. Any song, sermon, prayer, or experience that draws attention away from God and focuses the spotlight on the worshiper has missed the mark completely. Any authentic worship experience should leave us saying, "I hope God knows how much we appreciate Him."[6]

Genuine Worship Is Corporate as Well as Individual

Again, I realize this idea runs counter to cultural thinking. "I don't have to come to a church to worship God. I can express my admiration for God while on a camping trip, on the golf course, or in the kitchen as I wash dishes." You'll get no argument from me about that. The Bible compares every Christian to a temple in which the Holy Spirit dwells. We should be constantly worshiping God as we go through the activities of our lives, and we can do that anywhere.

However, to continue the sports analogy a moment, couldn't

the University of Kentucky basketball fans have expressed their appreciation for their team privately instead of collectively? Why go to all the time, trouble, and expense of a public celebration in a stadium?

Russell says, even though we Christians are like thousands of little lights trying to illuminate the world, there needs to be a time when all the little lights come together to recharge their batteries and become one giant floodlight that illuminates our great God.[7] God understood from the beginning of time our need to join other believers in worship. In the days of the Old Testament, prior to the building of the tabernacle and the temple, God commanded His people to assemble together at worship centers that He had designated such as Shechem, Shiloh, and Bethel. Later, God commanded the construction of the tabernacle and then the temple where the Israelites could come together for worship. In Acts 2, even after the arrival of the Holy Spirit, we find the apostles continuing to worship together. And today, God continues to encourage us not to forsake our own assembling together (see Hebrews 10:25).

Why is corporate worship so important? I believe God commands it, not primarily for His benefit, but for ours. Pastor Leith Anderson expressed our need for corporate worship this way:

> It is easy to lose hope, become pessimistic, and convince ourselves of defeat... But as Christians we must open our eyes to see the view from where Jesus sits... When I am discouraged and my hope runs thin, I remember that I am part of something much bigger than I am.[8]

Genuine Worship Is Active, Not Passive

In her thought-provoking book *Up with Worship*, Anne Ortlund described this scene from her childhood:

When I was little I used to play church with my friends. We'd get the chairs into rows, fight over who'd be preacher, vigorously lead the hymn singing, and generally have a great carnal time.

The aggressive kids wanted to be up front directing or preaching. The quieter ones were content to sit and be entertained by the up-fronters.

Occasionally we'd get mesmerized by the true sensationalistic crowd-sawyer—like the girl who said, "Boo! I'm the Holy Ghost!" But in general, if the up-fronters were good, they could hold their audience quite a while. If they weren't so good, eventually the kids would drift off to play something else—like jump rope or jacks.

That generation of children has now grown up, but most of them haven't changed too much. Every Sunday they still play church. They line up in rows for the entertainment. If it's pretty good, their church grows. If it's not too hot, eventually they'll drift off to play something else—like yachting or wife swapping.[9]

And drifting away they are in record numbers. In his book *Exit Interviews: Revealing Stories of Why People Are Leaving the Church*, William Hendricks reported that, not surprisingly, many people cited "boredom" as a major reason they quit attending worship services. However, as Hendricks probed further with those who had given up on church, he concluded, "I did not hear this as a call for more entertainment, but for more participation."[10]

The first-century church was not a spiritual entertainment center where members sat in pews staring at the backs of one another's heads while paid professionals put on the best show they could muster. Instead, every Christian actively participated in worship. In 1 Corinthians 14:26, Paul pulls back the curtain a bit and allows us to catch a glimpse of what the services were like in the early church:

> What is the outcome then, brethren? When you assemble, each one has a psalm, has a teaching, has a revelation, has a tongue, has an interpretation. Let all things be done for edification.

Don't allow the words *revelation* and *tongue* to cause you to miss the bigger principle. While interesting to debate, whether the gift of tongues is applicable for today or whether God is continuing to give revelation to His people apart from the Bible is not the point here. Worship involved the *active participation of the entire congregation,* not just the apostles and (later) the elders.

How do we pull that off today? We need to be careful to avoid the extremes. Some people are calling for a complete overhaul of Sunday morning worship services, moving away from what is termed "presentational worship" to more "participatory worship." One who advocates such a shift writes:

> Today's churches are built around the Sunday morning service, which is a spectator event. For laymen, participation is not allowed, except in the sense that a fan of pro football is participating in the game he watches and cheers for from the sidelines.
>
> Laymen aren't supposed to worship actively, but to maintain "an attitude of worship." That means being quiet and worshiping vicariously, if at all. If one of them stood up and said, "Great is the LORD and greatly to be praised!" the nearest usher would shut him up pronto.
>
> Suppose you're a layman, and you've just soared through the best week of your life. You arrive at church

dancing on air, bursting to share your good fortune with
your whole Christian family. Sorry. The format of the service doesn't allow for sharing, period.…

If the Lord puts a message on the pastor's heart, he can
deliver it to the church—in a sermon.… But if the Lord
puts a message on a layman's heart, what can he do?[11]

While I empathize with the writer's frustration, I don't agree
with the implied remedy—deemphasizing preaching ("too presentational") in favor of congregational sharing. As we will see in a
moment, biblical instruction from those God has selected as pastors and teachers is an important function of the church. But if the
paid professionals are the *only* ones doing the talking, how can we
ever hope to make worship participatory? Let me offer a few suggestions to church members as well as church leaders:

1. *Utilize small groups in your congregation.* The above writer
   is correct in many respects. There *should* be a time when
   members can share their excitement over what God is
   doing in their lives or request prayer for special needs. If
   God has given them a unique insight into Scripture,
   there needs to be venue through which they can share
   that revelation. But why must we limit such participation
   to eleven o'clock on Sunday mornings? One of the values
   of small-group Bible studies such as Sunday school or
   home fellowship groups is that they provide an outlet for
   active participation.

2. *Create special worship services that encourage active participation.* "But isn't there value in the whole church assembling together and participating in worship rather than
   limiting participation to small groups?" Absolutely. That
   is why in our church we create special worship times in

addition to the Sunday morning services that emphasize congregational participation. Last night about eight hundred of our people came together for dinner. After we sang a few songs, I asked our members to share how God was working in their lives. I must admit that due to my lack of faith that people would have anything to share, I had "primed the pump" by preparing a few members ahead of time in case the service began to drag. But when I asked for volunteers, so many hands shot up that we didn't have a chance to get to all the "spontaneous" testimonies I had planned! We scatter four of these special services throughout the year, and our members can't wait for them.

3. *Actively participate in "passive" worship.* Just because you may not be one of the "up-fronters" as Anne Ortlund calls them—singing the solo, voicing the prayer, or preaching the sermon—you don't have to limit yourself to spectator status in worship. Commit to taking an active part in each portion of the service. When someone prays aloud, pray silently in your heart, agreeing with the one who is praying. When the congregation is singing, make sure you are singing as well, offering the song as your personal gift of praise to God. When the pastor is preaching, open your Bible to the passage and read along with him. Take notes on the message. (Hint to pastors: Providing outlines of your messages to your members will encourage them to take notes and remember what they have heard.)

The Danish theologian Sören Kierkegaard once observed that most people believe that in worship the pastor is the actor, the congregation is the audience, and God is the prompter reminding people of their lines. But in authentic worship, God is the audience, the congregation is the actor, and the pastor is simply the prompter reminding the people of their lost lines. Authentic worship is active, not passive.

Jesus told the woman He met at the well that God the Father was actively seeking people who would worship Him (John 4:23). Worship—magnifying God—should be a priority for every believer. And while we can and should worship God individually, it is an activity that is best performed in community.

INSTRUCTION

The early church not only engaged in worship, but they also committed themselves to "the apostles' teaching." Actually, I have just set up a false dichotomy that is far too common today between "worship" and "teaching." Worship is spiritual, we are led to believe, while teaching is cerebral; worship reaches the heart, while teaching reaches only the head.

Yet Jesus taught that there is an inseparable link between the worship of God and the Word of God. Consider again the story of Jesus' encounter with the Samaritan woman. She tried to divert Jesus' attention from her own sticky moral situation by posing a question about worship. In her day there was a raging debate about where to worship: in the Samaritan temple on Mount Gerizim or the Jewish temple in Jerusalem. If she were posing a similar question today, she might say, "Tell me, Jesus, does God prefer contemporary or traditional worship music?"

But Jesus refused to get in the middle of the worship war of His day and instead cut to the heart of the issue:

> But an hour is coming, and now is, when the true worshipers will worship the Father in spirit and truth; for such people the Father seeks to be His worshipers. God is spirit, and those who worship Him must worship in *spirit and truth*. (John 4:23-24)

God is looking for people whose worship flows from genuine desire rather than from ritualistic duty. Authentic worship involves a wellspring of emotion from our innermost being—our spirit. But such worship must be based on truth about God that is revealed in the Word of God. John Stott wrote:

> Word and worship belong indissolubly to each other. All worship is an intelligent and loving response to the revelation of God, because it is the adoration of his Name. Therefore acceptable worship is impossible without preaching. For preaching is making known the Name of the Lord, and worship is praising the Name of the Lord made known. Far from being an alien intrusion into worship, the reading and preaching of the word are actually indispensable to it. The two cannot be divorced.[12]

"Robert, I agree that the Word of God is important. But I read and study the Bible regularly. Why do I need a preacher in a church to communicate biblical truth? Isn't every Christian a 'priest' himself?" Certainly, one of the benefits of the indwelling Holy Spirit is that we have our own Private Tutor who explains and illuminates God's Word to us. But this does not eliminate our need to sit under the instruction of those whom God has selected and gifted to teach the Bible. Just as Christ has given each individual Christian a spiritual gift to use, He has also given every congregation spiritually gifted people:

> He gave some as apostles, and some as prophets, and some as evangelists, and some as pastors and teachers, for the equipping of the saints for the work of service, to the building up of the body of Christ; until we all attain to the unity of the faith, and of the knowledge of the Son of God, to a

mature man, to the measure of the stature which belongs to
the fullness of Christ. (Ephesians 4:11-13)

God is in the "bodybuilding" business. He is your Personal
Trainer who is absolutely dedicated to your spiritual development.
His job is not complete until you perfectly resemble His Son, Jesus
Christ, in your attitudes, actions, and affections. But God does not
accomplish this task by Himself. Paul is saying here that God has
hired some assistants within His spiritual gymnasium (the church)
to accomplish His goal for your life. Among them are "pastor-
teachers" (one word in the Greek language). Athletes who are serious about their physical development don't train in a vacuum.
They listen to the advice of their trainers. In the same way, Christians who are serious about their spiritual development realize the
value of training under the direction of those pastor-teachers God
has provided the church.

Nourishment

Dr. Luke tells us that another priority of that phenomenal first-
century church was the emotional nourishment of one another,
which he called "fellowship."

They were continually devoting themselves to the apostles'
teaching and to fellowship. (Acts 2:42)

What images come to your mind when you hear the word
fellowship? Too often we limit our idea of "fellowship" to the super-
ficial discussions that take place at church around the coffeepot or
in the hallway...

"Whadya think about the game yesterday?"

"Do you think the market is going up anytime soon?"

"How's everybody in your family?"

"How old do you think these doughnuts are?"

But as we read further in this passage from Acts, we find that Luke used the term *fellowship* to describe an absolute commitment these first-century believers had to the well-being of one another. They were so devoted to other believers that they were willing to sell their material possessions in order to take care of one another's financial needs.

Anne Ortlund writes that a church can be compared to either a bag of marbles or a bag of grapes. When marbles are shaken, they generate a lot of noise and create a lot of friction and nicks as they rub against one another. But when a bag of grapes is shaken, those grapes will start to mix together, ooze all over one another, and eventually become a part of one another.[13]

God intends for the church to be like a bag of grapes. Instead of bruising and banging against one another, God wants our lives to "ooze" into one another. We need the spiritual "juice" that comes from other Christians. Or, to switch metaphors, as a part of the body of Christ, we each need the spiritual energy that flows to us from other parts of the body. Just as a branch severed from a tree will die or an arm cut off from the body will wither away, Christians who are not connected to a body of believers are doomed to spiritual failure.

What do other Christians give us that we cannot provide for ourselves? The writer of Hebrews answered that question:

> Let us consider how to stimulate one another to love
> and good deeds, not forsaking our own assembling
> together, as is the habit of some, but encouraging one
> another; and all the more, as you see the day drawing
> near. For if we go on sinning willfully after receiving the
> knowledge of the truth, there no longer remains a sacrifice
> for sins. (10:24-26)

Challenge When We Are Complacent

The word *stimulate* means "to provoke or irritate." It is the same word used in Ephesians 6:4, "Fathers, do not provoke your children to anger" (my daughters' favorite verse in the Bible). Paul warned parents not to unnecessarily exasperate their children by being too critical or overbearing.

But here, the writer of Hebrews used the word positively. Just as a grain of sand acts as an irritant in an oyster to produce a pearl, other Christians may act as spiritual irritants to help produce the priceless image of Christ in our lives. Through positive interaction with other believers, we are challenged to a deeper relationship with God as we observe their responses in difficult situations or listen to their words of instruction and encouragement.

Other times it is through the experience of being involved with other Christians in a church that we are challenged to develop the virtues of patience, mercy, servanthood, and forgiveness. (Why is it that the church seems to contain more of these kinds of "irritants" than do other places?) Positively or negatively, other Christians motivate us to grow.

Encouragement When We Are Discouraged

"Not forsaking our own assembling together, as is the habit of some, but encouraging one another" (Hebrews 10:25). This past week I have been involved with three families who are each watching one of their own die from a terminal illness: a mother of two young boys, a father who was just preparing to enjoy his golden years of retirement, and a senior citizen who was sure he had many more years of life left. In each case, both the patients and the families have said to me, "We do not know how we could survive this ordeal if it were not for the love, prayers, and care of our church family."

I have been encouraged by the way church members have

bathed these families in prayer, written numerous notes of encouragement, provided an endless number of meals, and taken up
collections to pay for the innumerable medical bills. God has created the church to be a support system for times when we are discouraged.

And yet, amazingly, too many people allow sickness, financial
need, or marital problems to drive them away from the church at
just the time they most need it. One writer observed:

> Our faith isn't a luxury intended for periods of smooth sail-
> ing—neither is our fellowship. When trouble comes along,
> that's when it's wonderful to be part of a faithful, Bible-
> believing body of people who will rally around you. They'll
> pray for you, support you with their resources, encourage
> you, and counsel you in the tough decisions. The devil
> is the only one whose opinion is that you should take a
> sabbatical from church in hard times.[14]

Correction When We Stray

The writer of Hebrews was addressing a group of Christians who
were in serious danger of drifting away from their spiritual moor-
ings. He offered no hope for those who continued "sinning will-
fully after receiving the knowledge of the truth," but he did offer
an antidote to continued disobedience: "Don't forsake assembling
together." One of Satan's oldest and most effective strategies is to
isolate us from other Christians—and then destroy us. As Dietrich
Bonhoeffer wrote:

> Sin demands to have a man by himself. It withdraws him
> from the community. The more isolated a person is, the
> more destructive will be the power of sin over him, and the
> more deeply he becomes involved in it, the more disastrous

is his isolation. Sin wants to remain unknown. It shuns the light. In the darkness of the unexpressed it poisons the whole being of a person.[15]

We need other people who love us enough to confront and correct us when we begin to drift spiritually. Do you have people in your life who are willing to focus God's spotlight in the dark corners of your life? Do they have the intestinal fortitude to tell you the truth, no matter how much it hurts? I look back with both pain and gratitude as I recall various people in different congregations who were willing to point out deficiencies in my life that threatened my ministry, my marriage, or my relationship with God. I deeply appreciate the shrewd wisdom of Proverbs 27:6: "Faithful are the wounds of a friend, but deceitful are the kisses of an enemy."

SHARING

Imagine going to the gas station and filling your tank with gas. After you replace the nozzle and screw the gas cap back on, you climb back into your car and…just sit there. *It sure feels good to have a full tank of gas,* you reflect. *I want to relax and enjoy the sensation of a full tank for a while.*

Obviously, the only reason you place fuel in your car is so that you can go somewhere! The same is true about the spiritual fuel—worship, instruction, and nourishment (fellowship)—we receive at church.

Remember Paul's words in Ephesians 4:12? The purpose of the church is the "equipping of the saints for the work of service, to the building up of the body of Christ." The Greek word for *equip* refers to the loading of a ship with supplies before it sets out on a long journey—much like filling a car with gasoline. The reason we assemble together on Sundays is to receive the spiritual supplies we need for our journey into the world the other six days of the week. But it is not a sightseeing journey we are stocking up for. It is a voyage with a purpose: "to the building up of the body of Christ."

The word translated *building up* originally referred to the building of a house. Jesus Christ is in the business of building a spiritual temple for Himself composed not of bricks but of the lives of individuals who have committed themselves to Him. And we are the workmen who are to go out and gather those spiritual "bricks."

The early church understood this responsibility. They were not content just to sit and soak in the apostles' teaching, to engage in stirring worship, or to encourage one another in difficult times. They then "took it to the streets," sharing the gospel of Jesus Christ with anyone and everyone.

What happens to a church that is involved in worship, instruction, and nourishment but refuses to engage in sharing the gospel with others? Max Lucado answered that question by recounting a fishing trip he and his best friend, Mark, took with Max's dad over spring break from high school. Unfortunately, inclement weather kept them from fishing. Instead, they spent several days cooped up inside the cabin perusing old copies of *Reader's Digest* and playing endless rounds of Monopoly.

> I began to notice a few things I hadn't seen before. I noticed that Mark had a few personality flaws. He was a bit too cocky about his opinions. He was easily irritated and constantly edgy. He couldn't take any constructive criticism. Even though his socks did stink, he didn't think it was my business to tell him…. Dad couldn't do anything right; I wondered how someone so irritable could have such an even-tempered son. We sat in misery the whole day…. I learned a hard lesson that week. Not about fishing, but about people. When those who are called to fish don't fish,

they fight. When energy intended to be used outside is used inside, the result is explosive. Instead of casting nets, we cast stones.[16]

The first-century believers decided to expend their energy fishing for converts rather than fighting with congregants. The result? "The Lord was adding to their number day by day those who were being saved" (Acts 2:47).

Good Questions

I realize we have covered a lot of ground in this chapter, and thank you for staying with me. Let's wrap up by distilling these pages into two brief principles.

First, *we should view the church as God's creation instead of our organization.* Jesus Christ both created and selected the church to accomplish His purpose on earth. This means that involvement in a local body of believers is a necessity for every obedient disciple of Christ. Yes, the church is filled with imperfect people (you and me, for example) who often cause unnecessary stress and create unbelievable messes. But as my friend Howard Hendricks says, "The church is a lot like Noah's ark. If it weren't for the storm on the outside, you couldn't stand the stench on the inside."

Second, *we should choose a church that is based on God's principles instead of our preferences.* The four main functions of the church described in Acts 2—worship, instruction, nourishment, and sharing—outline a solid checklist regarding our choice of a church. Here are some good questions you might ask before choosing to join (or leave) a congregation:

- Is the Bible the foundation of the pastor's message as well as of all the teaching in the church?

- Does the music direct my attention toward God or toward the performers on stage?
- Does the church offer small-group opportunities for everyone in my family to grow spiritually and to fellowship with other Christians?
- Does the church earnestly pray for the physical, emotional, and spiritual needs of hurting people?
- Is there an active evangelism and missions program dedicated to taking the gospel of Christ beyond the four walls of the church?
- Is there something supernatural taking place in this church that can only be explained by the power of the Holy Spirit?

In his book *Great Church Fights,* Leslie Flynn compared Christians to two porcupines in the freezing north country of Canada that huddled together to keep warm. But because they were pricked by each other's quills, they moved apart. Soon they were shivering again and had to lie side by side for their own survival. They needed each other even though they needled each other!

To paraphrase John Donne's words, no Christian is an island unto himself. God has wired each of us so that we need one another—even though we often needle one another. The church is not a necessary evil, but a divine creation to provide the worship, instruction, nourishment, and ministry opportunities that are essential to experiencing more of God's power.

Eight

FLAMETHROWERS VS.
FIRE EXTINGUISHERS

Avoiding the Four "Spirit Quenchers"

My grandfather spent most of his life in a small town of less than five thousand people. One of the numerous stories I remember hearing from him concerned a rash of fires that occurred in his town within the space of just a few months. On a regular basis, the slumbering residents of the community would be awakened to the shrill sound of the fire alarms signaling that a house or business was engulfed in flames. Fortunately, the town had a dedicated fire chief who quickly mobilized his firefighters to extinguish the fires that continually threatened the city.

One night my grandfather's telephone rang, awakening him from a deep sleep. The caller informed my grandfather that his dry goods business was on fire. My grandfather quickly dressed and raced to his business. Fortunately, the fire department was already there, and my grandfather "worked the hose" with the fire chief in an effort to salvage the business he had poured his life into.

Not long afterward the cause of all of these random fires was discovered. Faulty wiring? A group of delinquent teenagers? No, the source of the fires was the fire chief himself! This pyromaniac would secretly start the fires and then work to extinguish them. (I suppose that's one way to keep yourself busy in a sleepy town.) One can hardly imagine a more bizarre scene than a man working feverishly to extinguish a fire that he was responsible for igniting…until we take a moment and look at our own lives.

In our time together, we have been addressing the question, "How do I ignite the fire of God's Spirit in my life so that I can experience more of His supernatural power?" A fire needs both heat and energy in order to burn. As we saw earlier, every Christian already possesses the "heat" (the presence of God's Holy Spirit). But that heat also needs fuel in order to burn. In the past three chapters, we have looked at three spiritual "combustibles" the Holy Spirit uses in our lives:

- the energy from the Word of God (the Bible);
- the energy from communication with God (prayer); and
- the energy from the people of God (the church).

Tragically, however, once the fire of God's Spirit begins to burn within us, we often grab the fire extinguisher and douse the flame that we (and God) have worked so hard to ignite. It is that ironic reality that the apostle Paul referred to in 1 Thessalonians 5:19 when he commanded:

Do not quench the Spirit.

The word *quench* means "to put out a fire" or "to cool." I never will forget the summer I was twelve years old when my dad and I took a motorcycle trip from Texas to South Dakota—in the middle of July. One of my most vivid memories of that trip is roaring through the forsaken terrain of northwest Texas (where thirty years later I find myself living) under the blistering heat of the midsummer sun. My dad was one of those fathers who never saw the need to stop for such frivolous activities as eating or using the rest room.

But this particular afternoon even he couldn't stand the heat any longer. We pulled our motorcycle into a little café out in the middle of nowhere, went inside, and ordered the largest glass of iced tea on the menu. More than thirty years later, I still remember the sensation of that cold liquid bringing relief to my parched throat, quenching my thirst.

But sometimes thirst can be a good thing, as in one's thirst for God. Unfortunately, we often quench our thirst for Him by extinguishing the fire of His Spirit working in our lives. How? In this chapter, we are going to look at four "Spirit quenchers" we must avoid if we desire to keep the fire of God's power burning within us.

Spirit Quencher No. 1: Immorality

Perhaps you have heard the story of the little boy being quizzed by his mother about the pastor's sermon. "Johnny, what did the pastor preach about today?"

"Sin," Johnny answers confidently.

"And what did the pastor say about sin?"

After a thoughtful moment, Johnny replies, "I think he was against it."

Make no mistake about it, God is against sin—all sin. It is not just the major infractions such as murder or grand theft that alienate us from God. "Minor" infractions such as pride, dishonesty, or gluttony are equally abhorrent in God's eyes. James tells us, "For whoever keeps the whole law and yet stumbles in one point, he has become guilty of all" (2:10).

While all sin has the same potential consequence in the next life—eternal separation from God—not all sins have the same consequences in this life. No one ever went to prison for harboring hateful thoughts about a coworker. No one ever sat in the electric chair for cheating on his income tax.

In fact, all sins do not even have the same effect on our relationship with God in this life. While it is popular to say, "God does not grade sin," the fact is that He does! God views sexual immorality differently from any other kind of sin we commit. If you have trouble accepting that, consider Paul's teaching in 1 Corinthians 6:

> Flee immorality. Every other sin that a man commits is outside the body, but the immoral man sins against his own body. Or do you not know that your body is a temple of the Holy Spirit who is in you, whom you have from God, and that you are not your own? (verses 18-19)

Paul asserted that immorality is unlike any other kind of sin. How so? Certainly there are physical and relational consequences of immorality that distinguish it from other kinds of wrongdoing. It's impossible to contract a life-threatening illness like AIDS through pride. It's quite rare for a wife to leave her husband simply because he is addicted to football on television. But sexual immorality results in unique and devastating consequences.

However, Paul's focus was not on the physical or relational effects of immorality, but on the unique spiritual consequence. There is a direct link, Paul asserted, between the practice of immorality and the presence of the Holy Spirit in our lives.

Warning: I am about to paint a disgusting mental picture to help you understand this passage. Take a deep breath and stay with me, and remember it's only an illustration: Imagine watching your mate or your teenage child having sex with another person. Are you repulsed by such a thought? Can you imagine yourself staying in the room for one moment while such a revolting act took place? Only the sickest of all voyeurs would derive any pleasure from such an activity.

But consider what we do if we indulge in sexual immorality.

The Greek term *porneia* found in 1 Corinthians 6 is a general term that could include adultery, lust, fornication, masturbation, or homosexuality. Because the Holy Spirit resides within us, if we engage in any kind of sexual immorality, we not only ask the Holy Spirit to *watch* what we are doing, we actually ask Him to *participate* with us in our lewd thoughts and acts.

How do you think the Holy Spirit responds to such an invitation?

Paul was saying that the Holy Spirit refuses to be a party to any kind of immorality. He is not about to hang around while we participate in the deeds of darkness. This is not to suggest that the Christian who engages in immoral behavior loses the indwelling of the Holy Spirit, as we discussed in chapter 2. But in a practical sense, I believe Paul was saying that immorality *quenches the Spirit's power* in our lives.

You probably have read or heard about recent studies indicating that the percentage of Christians who practice immorality is no lower than that of non-Christians. *Could this disturbing statistic help explain why so few Christians experience the power of God's Spirit in their daily lives?*

What is the remedy to immoral behavior? Paul said it begins with the realization that "you are not your own...you have been bought with a price" (1 Corinthians 6:19-20). The word translated *bought* is a term that means "to be purchased from the slave market." In Paul's day, slaves were treated like animals or tools. They would be brought in chains to the slave market where they would be placed on the trading block as potential buyers prodded and poked them as one might inspect a slab of meat before purchase. The highest bidder would then lead the slave from the trading block in chains and take him to his home where the owner was free to treat—or mistreat—the slave in any way he desired. If he wanted to slit the slave's throat, he was free to do so. The slave was nothing but a piece of property.

Paul reminds us that every one of us was a slave of sin. We were in bondage to Satan with no hope and no possible way of escape. All that awaited us was a lifetime of misery as we awaited our final and eternal execution. But God, for no other reason than His inexplicable love for us, looked down on our plight and sent His Son, Jesus Christ, to pay the necessary price to redeem us for Himself.

While he was still a congressman from Illinois, Abraham Lincoln heard about a slave auction in a nearby community and decided to attend so that he might witness this barbaric practice for himself. He watched as a young girl was being auctioned off to the highest bidder. Unable to restrain himself, Lincoln entered the bidding war. After continually being challenged to raise his offer, Lincoln's bid prevailed, and the young girl was brought to him.

"You're free" Lincoln told her.

With her head bowed, the girl mumbled, "I'm sorry, sir, but I don't know what that means."

Lincoln said, "It means you can do whatever you want to do, you can say whatever you want to say, and you can go wherever you want to go."

The girl raised her head and, with tears streaming down her face, said, "Then, sir, I'll go with you."

You are not your own; you have been bought with a price. Before we engage in any kind of immoral behavior, we need to stop and remember the price—the steep price—that Christ paid in order to set us free from the slavery of sin.

Spirit Quencher No. 2: Bitterness

Not long ago I stood outside a hospital room talking with a man about his wife's cancer. "The doctor opened her up and discovered that the tumor's tentacles had wrapped themselves around several vital organs, making it impossible to remove the tumor," he explained to me. The tumor was literally strangling the life out of the woman. The author of Hebrews used similar imagery to explain what bitterness does to us: "See to it that no one comes short of the grace of God; that no root of bitterness springing up causes trouble, and by it many be defiled" (12:15).

Sooner or later (probably sooner) every one of us is going to be hurt—deeply hurt—by someone else. It may be a friend who betrays us, a pastor who disappoints us, a business associate who cheats us, or a mate who deserts us. Offenses in life are inevitable. But every hurt we experience in life is accompanied by a supernatural outpouring of grace from the Holy Spirit to heal that hurt. If we refuse that gift of grace and decide to hold on to the offense, our anger will eventually metastasize into a tumor of bitterness that strangles our relationship with other people and with God. Lewis Smedes describes how bitterness, like cancer, works silently but nevertheless powerfully:

> We make believe we are at peace while the furies rage
> within, beneath the surface. There, hidden and suppressed,
> our hate opens the subterranean faucets of venom that will
> eventually infect all of our relationships in ways we cannot
> predict.[1]

One reason I speak and write about forgiveness so frequently and passionately is because of the devastating consequences of unforgiveness I see every day. I have watched bitterness destroy friendships, families, and entire congregations. Bitterness quenches the supernatural grace the Holy Spirit provides us to handle the unintentional slights or the premeditated attacks that come from other people.

How do we avoid the trap of bitterness that short-circuits the supernatural working of the Spirit in our lives?

REALIZE THAT OFFENSES ARE INEVITABLE

Will you allow this thought to sink in for a moment, because it really is a liberating truth: *You cannot control anyone except yourself.* We waste so much energy trying to induce, prevent, or alter other people's thoughts and actions. But ultimately we cannot keep our boss from firing us, our mate from leaving us, or our children from rebelling against us.

The writer of Hebrews treats mistreatment by others as a *fait accompli*. He simply warns that *when*—not *if*—someone hurts you, make sure you do not allow that offense to take root in your spirit. You cannot control other people, but you *can* control your response to other people.

REFLECT ON GOD'S FORGIVENESS OF YOU

There is an inseparable link between receiving and granting forgiveness. Simply put, you cannot give away what you have not received. Only when you truly understand the tremendous debt God has forgiven you will you ever be motivated to forgive other people. The parable in Matthew 18 concerning the slave who had been released of a six-billion-dollar debt but refused to forgive a fellow slave his sixteen-dollar debt illustrates the hypocrisy of our unforgiveness. Forgiveness is the obligation of the forgiven.

RELEASE YOUR OFFENDER FROM HIS OBLIGATION TO YOU

The word *forgive* means "to release." When I forgive someone, I am not denying the reality of his offense or the severity of the hurt he has caused. Instead, forgiveness is a deliberate choice that says, "What _____ did to me was wrong and hurt me deeply. But today I am releasing him of any obligation he has to me, not because he deserves to be forgiven or has even asked to be forgiven.

I am forgiving him because of the forgiveness I have received from Jesus Christ."

REMEMBER THE CONSEQUENCES OF UNFORGIVENESS

The Matthew 18 parable ends with the king sentencing the unforgiving slave to the torture chamber until he repays to the king everything that is owed. Is Jesus insinuating that if we refuse to forgive others, God is going to rescind His forgiveness of us? Of course not. Jesus is saying that if we find it impossible to forgive another person, it may be because we have never received God's forgiveness in our own life. And if we continue in unforgiveness, we are sentencing ourselves to our own private torture chamber of bitterness.

Perhaps you saw the movie or read the book about Rubin "Hurricane" Carter, the boxer who was wrongly convicted of three murders and spent twenty years in prison paying for someone else's crime. Certainly anyone suffering such an injustice would be a candidate for justifiable bitterness. But Carter chose a different response:

> The question invariably arises, it has before and it will again: "Rubin, are you bitter?" And in answer to that I say, "After all that's been said and done—the fact that the most productive years of my life, between the ages of twenty-nine and fifty, have been stolen; the fact that I was deprived of seeing my children grow up—wouldn't you think I would have a right to be bitter? Wouldn't anyone under those circumstances have a right to be bitter? In fact, it would be very easy to be bitter. But that has never been my nature, or my lot, to do things the easy way. If I have learned nothing else in my life, I've learned that bitterness only consumes the vessel that contains it. And for me to permit bitterness

to control or to infect my life in any way whatsoever would be to allow those who imprisoned me to take even more than the 22 years they've already taken. Now that would make me an accomplice to their crime.[2]

Rubin "Hurricane" Carter carefully calculated the cost of unforgiveness and decided he was unwilling to pay.

SPIRIT QUENCHER NO. 3: GREED

I have a friend who as a teenager felt God's call to serve as a medical missionary. My friend possessed a natural ability in science (while I was one of those who could never see *anything* under a microscope) and a passion to use his abilities to share the gospel of Jesus Christ in a foreign land. After my friend graduated from college, he married and entered medical school. But as he began to consider the incredible amounts of money he could make as a physician, his interest in missions began to wane, and finally, it died. He had plenty of rationalizations for his change of heart:

"Maybe it was just teenage hormones instead God's calling I was feeling."

"I can still be active in kingdom business by teaching Bible studies in my church and witnessing to my patients."

"I will use some of the money I earn to invest in God's work and send others to the mission field."

While any and all of my friend's excuses may be legitimate, I believe the real reason for his change of heart was the love of money. While immorality quenches the Holy Spirit's presence in our lives, and bitterness quenches the Spirit's love in our lives, greed can actually *extinguish* the Spirit's purpose in our lives. How so?

As we saw in chapter 4, God has one overriding purpose for every Christian: to be transformed into the image of His Son, Jesus

Christ. But God also has a unique plan for our individual lives that He communicates to us through His Holy Spirit. "For it is God who is at work within you, giving you the will and the power to achieve his purpose" (Philippians 2:13, Phillips).

God's Spirit may be creating a desire within you to go to the mission field. Or He may be leading you to get married. He may tell you it is time to have a child. He may be prompting you to give some money to a friend who has a financial need. Or He may be encouraging you to take your wife away for a long weekend to rekindle your relationship.

Right now, Paul says, the Holy Spirit is creating in you a desire to obey Him. But nothing will extinguish that flame more quickly than being overly concerned about money.

I am not suggesting that we should never consider our financial situation before we make a decision. Jesus reminds us that a wise person "counts the cost" before jumping into a project. But there is a vast difference between managing our money wisely and hoarding it. A person who is controlled by greed never believes he has enough money to follow those inner promptings of the Holy Spirit. He just cannot bring himself to let loose of his cash. "I'm saving my money for a rainy day" or "What if I run out of money?" are his common rationalizations for disobedience.

Jesus spoke about such a person in His familiar parable about the seed that fell on four types of soil. Each soil represents four conditions of the human heart onto which the seed (the Word of God) falls. Some of the seed

> fell among the thorns, and the thorns came up and choked
> them out.… The one on whom seed was sown among the
> thorns, this is the man who hears the word, and the worry
> of the world and the deceitfulness of wealth choke the
> word, and it becomes unfruitful. (Matthew 13:7,22)

Here Jesus described a person who hears God's voice clearly but allows a concern about money to prevent him from responding. What did Jesus mean by "the deceitfulness of wealth"? The person consumed by greed has bought into two myths about money:

Myth No. 1: Money will satisfy our deepest needs. The reason the greedy person is so unwilling to let go of his money is that he thinks in doing so he is giving up his ticket to satisfaction in life. But the reality is that no amount of money is sufficient to fill the vacuum of an empty life. Solomon, the wealthiest man of his day, lamented: "I collected for myself silver and gold and the treasure of kings and provinces.... And behold all was vanity and striving after wind and there was no profit under the sun" (Ecclesiastes 2:8,11).

Myth No. 2: Money will protect us from every adversity. "If I can just accumulate X amount of dollars, I'll be set for life. I will never have to worry about debt, sickness, accidents, or unemployment." Again, Solomon described such a person when he wrote, "The wealth of the rich is their fortified city; they *imagine* it an unscalable wall" (Proverbs 18:11, NIV). The key word in this passage is *imagine*. In truth, money can be easily lost through bad investments, unwise purchases, emergencies, or lawsuits. "Cast but a glance at riches, and they are gone, for they will surely sprout wings and fly off to the sky like an eagle," Solomon counseled in Proverbs 23:5 (NIV).

Even more important, no matter how much money we accumulate, we will never protect ourselves against inevitable death and judgment by God. Proverbs 11:4 underscores this truth: "Riches do not profit in the day of wrath."

KEEPING GREED AT BAY

How do we keep greed from extinguishing God's purpose and power in our lives?

First, we need to rise above our natural inclination to worship money by viewing money realistically. Despite everything we see and read around us, money's ability to satisfy and protect is really extremely limited.

Second, we need to hold on to money loosely. By this I do not mean spending money irresponsibly. Indeed, it is vital that we be good stewards by saving and investing regularly for future needs. But it is equally important that once we have set aside a reasonable amount of money—perhaps 10 to 15 percent of our income—we let go of the rest. The purpose of life is not to see how many green pieces of paper with dead presidents we can collect before we die. Money is simply a tool to help us enjoy life, provide for our families, and invest in God's eternal work. When opportunities to help others or enhance our relationships come along, we need to allow money to slip through our fingers more freely. When you feel a prompting to purchase that toy for your child, take a special trip with your mate, or give a special gift to your church, do it. Every time you obey such an impulse, you have won another victory over greed. By holding on to our money more loosely, we will also loosen its grip on our hearts.

Third, we need to be grateful for the money we do have. Expressing gratitude to God for our money has a way of reminding us that it all belongs to Him. This week our church received a large contribution from one of our members. When I thanked him for his generosity, he said, "It's not hard to give money away when you realize it is not yours to begin with."

SPIRIT QUENCHER NO. 4: WORRY

Does the following scenario sound familiar?

You finally start making progress in your relationship with God. As you become more aware of the working of His Spirit in your life, you begin to catch a glimpse of the fantastic possibilities that await you. The different facets of your life begin working with one another instead of against one another. You find it easier to get up in the morning and spend time with God. Your exercise routine becomes more consistent, giving you the energy you need to focus on your priorities. Consequently, you start experiencing greater success in your business and more fulfilling relationships with friends and family. Everything is working together beautifully for a few weeks…or a few days…until you are paralyzed by two little words that carry the same jolt as a 50,000-volt stun gun. *What if…*

> *I lose my job?*
> *I develop cancer?*
> *my children are killed in an accident?*
> *my mate has an affair?*

Suddenly, your desire to spend time with God, to exercise, to pursue your career goals, or to strengthen your marriage is gone. Instead, you are consumed by this paralyzing anxiety that you cannot shake no matter how hard you try.

E. Stanley Jones described fear as "the sand in the machinery of life."[3] We might paraphrase Jones's excellent word picture this way: "Fear is the sand in the working of God's Spirit."

On a very practical level, Chuck Swindoll defined worry as:

Anything that drains your tank of joy—something you cannot change, something you are not responsible for, something you are unable to control, something (or someone) that frightens and torments you, agitates you, keeps you awake when you should be asleep.[4]

We may be prone to think of worry as a minor issue compared to major sins such as immorality, bitterness, or greed. It isn't. Do you know what the most frequent command in the Bible is? It isn't "Fornicate not," "Hate not," or "Covet not." There are 365 verses in the Bible that command us to "Fear not." Our tendency toward anxiety is so powerful that God has to remind us 365 times—at least once a day—not to worry.

But overcoming worry is a lot easier said than done, isn't it? How can we keep worry from quenching the power of God's Spirit in our lives?

DETERMINE THE SOURCE OF YOUR FEAR

Identifying the cause of your anxiety is an important first step in conquering fear. Some potential sources of anxiety include:

1. *God.* God? This may seem strange to those who want to dismiss all fear as "satanic" by quoting 2 Timothy 1:7: "For God has not given us a spirit of fear" (NKJV). But if the Holy Spirit is residing in us, then we must believe that He is continually prompting us toward certain actions, as well as warning us against certain behaviors. A sudden desire to call a friend in a distant city, to check up on our teenager's whereabouts on a Friday night, to schedule an appointment with the doctor, or to avoid taking a planned trip out of town could originate with God for our good or for the benefit of someone important to us. But such concerns turn into fear only when we *dwell* on them instead of *act* on them.

2. *Fatigue.* Vince Lombardi once said, "Fatigue makes cowards of us all." I've noticed in my own life that I am most prone to irrational fear when I am physically or emotionally worn out. Consider Elijah, the Old Testament prophet who boldly confronted an evil king and conquered the 850 false prophets of Baal. Immediately following this major victory, Elijah fled for his life because of a single threat from one irate woman named Jezebel. After such a powerful victory, what suddenly caused Elijah to

become so fearful? He was hungry and exhausted. It took several servings of "angel food" cakes and a couple of naps before Elijah regained a realistic perspective about his situation. As my friend Howard Hendricks says, "Sometimes the most spiritual thing you can do is take a nap."

3. *Satan.* While we should not fall into the easy habit of blaming Satan for everything that goes wrong (sometimes it is nothing more than our own stupidity or self-absorption), the fact is that Satan is indeed responsible for many of the fearful thoughts that drift into our minds. Think for a moment about the things you have worried about in the last ten years. How many of those things ever happened? Not many, I suspect. Jesus described Satan as "a liar and the father of lies" (John 8:44). Satan loves to taunt us with the "what ifs." He encourages us to grab the reins of responsibility for our lives away from God by convincing us that we must look out for ourselves. Elisabeth Elliot reminds us that ultimately (and fortunately) we are not responsible for our future: "Today is mine. Tomorrow is none of my business. If I peer anxiously into the fog of the future, I will strain my spiritual eyes so that I will not see clearly what is required of me now."[5]

DECIDE TO CONFRONT YOUR FEAR

If you determine that your concern has no basis in reality and is simply an attempt by the Enemy to derail you, then dismiss it (we will discuss how to do that in a moment).

On the other hand, if you decide that your concern is legitimate, then act on it. For example, if you are concerned about your health, schedule an appointment with your doctor instead of brooding over what that unusual lump may represent. Instead of lying awake at night wondering if you have made the right investment decisions for your retirement, develop an informed plan with a financial advisor. Are you fearful that a distance is growing between you and your mate? After dinner tonight, talk with him or her about your concern and work together on a way to strengthen your relationship.

There is a vast difference between the legitimate concerns that God brings into our consciousness and the fear that originates with our Adversary. Godly concern leads to change and success; fear leads to paralysis and failure. Paul expressed that reality in his second letter to the Corinthian Christians:

> For the sorrow [concern] that is according to the will of
> God produces a repentance [change] without regret, leading
> to salvation, but the sorrow of the world produces death.
> (2 Corinthians 7:10)

Nothing will cause the fog of fear to dissipate more quickly than decisive action. Napoleon Hill once wrote, "Do the things you fear, and the death of fear is certain."[6]

DELIVER YOUR FEAR TO GOD

Even after you confront your anxiety head-on by taking decisive action, you may still find it difficult to shake recurring fears. When this happens, God encourages us to "[cast] all your anxiety upon Him, because He cares for you" (1 Peter 5:7).

Notice that little but crucial word *all.* God does not limit the size of the concern we turn over to Him. His shoulders are broad enough to handle our concerns about our health, our children, our finances, and our future. The late Corrie ten Boom used to say, "When I worry I go to the mirror and say to myself, 'This tremendous thing which is worrying me is beyond a solution. It is especially too hard for Jesus Christ to handle.' After I have said that, I smile and I am ashamed."

God is fully capable of shouldering your concerns, and He is fully willing to do so because He cares for you!

DO THE RIGHT THING

Immorality quenches the Spirit's presence.

Bitterness quenches the Spirit's power to handle our hurts.

Greed quenches the Spirit's promptings.

Worry quenches the Spirit's peace.

What is the antidote for the four Spirit quenchers we have discussed in this chapter? In a word, *obedience*. There is incredible spiritual energy that comes from simply obeying rather than stewing over the commands of God. Nothing will rekindle the power of God's Spirit in our lives any more quickly than doing what we know we should do.

Are there immoral relationships or habits that are grieving the Holy Spirit who resides within you? Forsake them.

Is there someone who has wounded you deeply? Forgive him.

Are you being strangled by greed? Flee from it.

Are you paralyzed by worry? "Do not fear, for I am with you" (Isaiah 41:10).

The great Puritan preacher Jonathan Edwards compiled a list of seventy resolutions that guided the course of his life. What was number twenty-five on his list should be number one on the list of anyone who is determined to be a flamethrower rather than a fire extinguisher: "To examine carefully and constantly what that one thing in me is, which causes me in the least to doubt the love of God; and so direct all my forces against it."[7]

I suspect you already know what that "one thing" is in your life that is quenching the power of God's Spirit. You have the power to change that one thing *right now.* Do it, and watch the flame of God's Spirit begin to burn brightly again in your life!

～

Dear heavenly Father:

In the stillness of this moment, I hear You once again speaking to me about this "one thing" that has been quenching the power of Your Spirit in my life. Lord, I'm tired—so tired—of the guilt that comes from my refusal to surrender to Your control over all of my life. I am asking You to help me realize the tremendous power You have given me already to say no and to continue to say no. Right now I resolve to be obedient to You in this area of my life. And if I should stumble again, I will refuse to give up or give in. Thank You for giving me both the resolve and the spiritual resources to say yes to You and no to the Evil One who continually attempts to govern my life. In the name and through the power of Jesus I pray. Amen.

Nine

BATTLE READY!

How to Win the Struggle Within

My friend Steve Lawson poses an interesting question: How would you react if while driving home from work you heard on the radio that a lion had escaped from the zoo—and was last spotted roaming one of the streets near your neighborhood?

Would you disregard the news alert? Would you change stations searching for soothing music instead of listening to an alarmist's warning?

Of course not! You would be on a heightened state of alert. You would call home and warn your family not to go outside. Your eyes would carefully scan the landscape until you had pulled into the driveway and were safely inside your home.[1]

Whether you realize it or not, a lion *is* loose, and it is stalking you relentlessly. This beast will not rest until he has destroyed you, along with everything and everyone precious to you. His name is Satan. The Bible says that he roams about like a "roaring lion, seeking someone to devour" (1 Peter 5:8)…and that someone is *you*.

Satan is far more dangerous than any animal that could do nothing more than kill you and thereby dispatch your soul to heaven.

Satan's goal for your life is the defilement of your conscience, the dissolution of your family, and the destruction of your effectiveness in God's kingdom.

While every Christian is a potential victim of Satan's attacks, I believe that those who are pursuing more in their relationship with God are of particular interest to the Enemy. The more the Holy Spirit releases His power in your life, the more Satan unleashes his attacks against your entire being. William Gurnall writes, "It is the image of God reflected in you that so enrages hell; it is this at which the demons hurl their mightiest weapons."[2]

If we are going to be successful in surviving the inevitable attacks of Satan and his minions, there are several things we need to understand about him.

SATAN'S REALITY

Maybe you remember the recurring character of "The Church Lady" from television's *Saturday Night Live*. Comedian Dana Carvey portrayed an eccentric old woman with a repulsive, judgmental personality who attributed everything that happens in life to Satan. Whenever she uttered her signature line, "Could it be... *SATAN?*" the audience roared with laughter.

What a brilliant strategy on the part of our enemy! If you were Satan, could you devise a better way to succeed in your covert operations than to make people think you don't exist, or at least transform your image into a laughable character such as a little red man with a tail and pitchfork whom no one takes seriously?

Interestingly, the Bible never attempts to prove Satan's existence but assumes it, just as it assumes the existence of God. Every writer of the New Testament mentions Satan. Nineteen of the twenty-seven books of the New Testament refer to him by one of his names. Jesus Christ spoke of Satan in twenty-five different references in the Gospels and had a face-to-face confrontation with him. If you believe the Bible, then you must believe in the existence of a personal devil.

SATAN'S ANGER

Satan is real, and he is also very angry. What's he so worked up about, you ask? He is enraged that God cast him out of heaven because of the pride uncovered in his heart when he served as God's chief angel. He is furious that he could not persuade all the other angels to follow him in his rebellion against God. He is irritated that his plan to destroy Christ backfired and resulted in the salvation of the very people he was trying to carry with him to hell. Satan is one frustrated creature!

But he is unwilling to go down without a fight. He is determined to deceive as many people as he can into following him instead of following God.

This means that from the moment we are born into this world, we are in the middle of a raging battle. As John Eldredge writes:

> Man is not born into a sitcom or a soap opera; he is born
> into a world at war. This is not *Home Improvement;* it's
> *Saving Private Ryan.* There will be many, many battles to
> fight on many different battlefields.[3]

The apostle Paul expressed the reality of our spiritual war this way:

> For our struggle is not against flesh and blood, but against
> the rulers, against the powers, against the world forces of

this darkness, against the spiritual forces of wickedness in
the heavenly places. (Ephesians 6:12)

The word translated *struggle* originally referred to a wrestling
match in which the loser had his eyes gouged out and was then
executed. (Can you imagine what matches like that would do for
the ratings of *World Wrestling Entertainment* today?) Paul said *every
one* of us is engaged in this life-and-death struggle whether we
realize it or not.

This world is not a playground on which to entertain ourselves; it is a battleground on which we are fighting for the survival
of our souls. The Christian who chooses to deny or simply ignore
that truth does so at his own peril. Martyn Lloyd-Jones reminds us:

> Not to realize that you are in a conflict means one thing
> only, and it is that you are so hopelessly defeated, and so
> "knocked out" as it were, that you do not even know it—
> you are unconscious! It means that you are completely
> defeated by the devil. Anyone who is not aware of a fight
> and a conflict in a spiritual sense is in a drugged and
> hazardous condition.[4]

SATAN'S METHODS

Not only is Satan real and angry (or real angry), but he is also
intentional. By that I mean that Satan has a very specific strategy
for the destruction of your marriage, your children, your career,
your peace of mind, and your relationship with God. In 2 Corinthians 2:11, Paul encourages us not to be ignorant of Satan's
"schemes" or, literally, his "methods." Like a master fisherman, the
Enemy uses a variety of bait to hook various kinds of "fish." Some
people are easily enticed by lust. Others, who might never fall into

an adulterous relationship, are lured away from God by ambition. Still others are pulled away by greed. Satan tailor-makes his temptations to coincide with our individual tastes.

Yet while his methods are varied, all of his temptations enter our lives in the very same way: through our minds. Adultery doesn't begin in the bedroom, ambition does not originate in a staff meeting, and greed doesn't start with a review of your quarterly 401(k) statement. All sin originates in the mind. Wrong thinking leads to wrong actions.

THE DILEMMA OF DOUBLE-MINDEDNESS

I imagine you purchased this book because you have an inner desire to experience more in your relationship with God. You are ready to pay any price, forsake any relationship, and begin any discipline necessary to unleash God's power in your life. Yet sooner or later (probably sooner), you are going to find yourself in the cross-currents of competing desires.

- You will want to read your Bible and pray, but you'll also want to watch that sitcom or read that novel.
- You will want to run from that dangerous relationship, but you'll also want to stay and see how things develop.
- You will want to give that financial gift to God's work, but you'll also want to keep your money in case of an emergency.
- You will want to wait on God's answer to your dilemma, but you'll also want to take matters into your own hands.

The Bible has a term for those competing desires we all possess. It's called being *double-minded*. The double-minded person, James wrote, is "unstable in all his ways" (1:8). In many ways he is the most miserable of all people because he cannot enjoy sin as much as the outright pagan does, but neither does he fully enjoy the benefits that come from a wholehearted commitment to God. François Fénelon described the dilemma of the double-minded this way:

> Woe to those weak and timid souls who are divided between God and their world! They want and they do not want. They are torn by desire and remorse at the same time.... They have a horror of evil and a shame of good. They have the pains of virtue without tasting its sweet consolations. O how wretched they are.[5]

These contradictory desires keep us from pursuing God's will with all of our energy. The key to conquering double-mindedness is to commit to a singleness of mind. I like Clifford Williams's description of the single-minded person:

> We possess singleness when we are not pulled in opposite directions and when we act without wanting something further for ourselves. Our inner drives do not conflict; they are aimed in one direction. The motives we appear to have are the ones we really have. Our inner focus is unified and our public posture corresponds with it. We are not, in short, divided.[6]

But how do we pull that off? What is the answer to those competing desires we all possess? While we will never be able to prevent Satan from dangling his bait in front of us, or to completely remove our old desires that cause us to want to snap at the bait, we *can* recognize and repudiate the lies Satan uses to lure us away from pursuing God with a singleness of mind. The pages that follow expose three of Satan's favorite lies that he uses to discourage us in our search of more in our relationships with God.

LIE NO. 1: "GOD HAS CONDEMNED ME, THEREFORE I AM REJECTED"

I normally do not counsel women, but Sandra Harrison desperately needed to see me, she said. With my office door open and my secretary nearby, Sandra told me of a shameful secret she had been carrying for years. Sandra had been a committed Christian since age nine, but as a high-school junior, she had started dating a boy she knew was not God's best choice for her. Within a few months she became pregnant, and her boyfriend immediately (and predictably) dumped her.

Her parents did not hesitate to take action. Her promising future, along with promised scholarships to a prestigious university, meant that Sandra could not have the child and disrupt the life her parents had planned. They insisted on an abortion.

Twenty years later Sandra still carries the guilt of that experience with her. She finds it impossible to read more than a sentence or two in the Bible or pray for any period of time without thinking about her sin. Every time she hears a message in church on "the sanctity of human life," she hears a single word whispered in her ear: *murderer*. Is she condemned to a lifetime of unrelenting guilt for her mistake?

I do not know you personally, but I'm almost certain I know one thing about you: Somewhere in your past is a wrong relationship, a bad choice, or simply a wasted opportunity that continues to haunt you. Every time you attempt to move forward in your walk with God, you find yourself reliving that signal event in your life. Although you desperately want more in your relationship with

God, you wonder, *Am I destined to a mediocre faith for the rest of my life because of the time that I _____?* If you have ever asked yourself that question or are still struggling with it, you are a victim of one of Satan's favorite and most powerful lies.

Guilt causes us to run away from, rather than run toward, the person we have wronged, doesn't it? For example, if you are delinquent in paying a debt, how likely are you to call your creditor and shoot the breeze with him? Or if you hear through the grapevine that a friend is angry with you for betraying a confidence, how anxious are you to meet your friend for coffee so that you can straighten out the mess? Guilty people tend to run, just as Adam and Eve ran from God in the garden.

All Satan must do to disrupt your relationship with God is convince you that God is still angry with you over some past mistake. Notice I said *still* angry. If you are not a Christian, then the reason you feel guilty is because you *are* guilty. The Bible says that God's anger burns continually against the unrighteous. But as we saw in chapter 4, when you became a Christian, God transferred His anger from you and poured it out on Jesus Christ: "He made Him [Jesus] who knew no sin to be sin on our behalf, so that we might become the righteousness of God in Him" (2 Corinthians 5:21).

The result is that that there is "no condemnation" awaiting those who belong to Christ Jesus, Paul assures us in Romans 8:1. God is not like an unforgiving spouse who continually dredges up his mate's past mistakes in order to keep the upper hand in the relationship. Instead, God casts our sins into the depths of the sea, and He remembers them no more.

Maybe this is a truth that you know intellectually but still have a difficult time accepting experientially. Every time you attempt to progress into a more intimate fellowship with God, Satan whispers in your ear, "Remember when you _____ ?" and stops

you cold in your tracks. *You're guilty. Unworthy. Condemned.*
What is the answer to this lie?

ACCEPT OUR OWN HUMANITY

At the risk of sounding flip about the very serious subject of sin, we all need to lighten up just a little. Face it, because of your predisposition to sin you are going to make mistakes—*big* mistakes. Wrong choices, broken commitments, missed opportunities, and wasted time are the remnants of the fallen nature we all possess. Brennan Manning reminds us of our humanity:

> When I get honest, I admit I am a bundle of paradoxes. I believe and I doubt, I hope and get discouraged. I love and I hate, I feel bad about feeling good, I feel guilty about not feeling guilty. I am trusting and suspicious. I am honest and I still play games. Aristotle said I am a rational animal; I say I am an angel with an incredible capacity for beer.
>
> To live by grace means to acknowledge my whole life story, the light side and the dark. In admitting my shadow side I learn who I am and what God's grace means.
>
> As Thomas Merton put it, "A saint is not someone who is good but who experiences the goodness of God."[7]

Do you realize that God is not nearly as surprised by your mistakes as you are? When you sin, God does not slap His forehead and exclaim, "I can't *believe* she did that!" Instead, as the psalmist wrote, God "knows our frame [and] is mindful that we are but dust." We are, indeed, human.

RECEIVE GOD'S FORGIVENESS

If you and I were absolutely perfect, then the death of Christ would have been totally unnecessary. But Christ gave His life not for our goodness, but for our badness. His excruciating death on the cross resulted in the forgiveness of not just some of our sins, but *all* of our sins. "He made you alive together with Him, having forgiven us all our transgressions" (Colossians 2:13).

Last night I was visiting with one of my closest friends who is preparing for his journey to heaven in just a few weeks. As he reflected over the course of his life, he said, "I have made so many mistakes, so many wrong choices. I have hurt God in so many ways." I was just about to interject some pastoral words of consolation. I didn't need to. He continued, "But praise the name of Jesus Christ who died for all of those sins."

Let me ask you a simple question. Which of your sins is too large to be covered by the grace of God?

- Immorality? Then Rahab the harlot would have been disqualified as an instrument of God to bring deliverance to Israel and to be a direct ancestor of Jesus Christ.
- Unbelief? Then Abraham, who had many lapses of faith, would have been disqualified from being the father of the Israelites and a friend of God.
- Adultery? Then David would have been disqualified from being the leader of Israel and a man after God's own heart.
- Blasphemy? Then Paul, who described himself as a "blasphemer and violent aggressor," would have been disqualified from being the world's greatest missionary.
- Murder? Then Moses, David, and Paul would have been disqualified from serving as the most influential leaders in the Old and New Testaments.
- Betrayal? Then Peter, who disavowed Christ three times within just a few hours, would have been disqualified as the leader of the first-century church.

Refuse to listen to the lie that your sins have condemned you to a mediocre relationship with God. It is for those sins—the ones that continue to haunt you—that Christ gave His life.

LIE NO. 2: "GOD HAS ABANDONED ME, THEREFORE I AM ALONE"

Betty, a young mother of three, is one of the most devout Christians I have ever known. When she was diagnosed with ovarian cancer six months ago, her first response was to call for the leaders of the church to come to her home and pray for her healing, which we did. But over these last months, the cancer has continued to spread throughout her body, resulting in indescribable pain. As I sat by her bed and held her hand, she said, "I'm still trusting God for a miracle." But there was a sadness in her eyes that communicated what she would never have articulated: a profound disappointment with God.

C. S. Lewis observed that "every war, every famine or plague, almost every death-bed, is the monument to a petition that was not granted."[8] I imagine that you can point to a time in your life—perhaps even right now—when you have struggled with the issue of unanswered prayer. You've asked God for...

- specific guidance about a decision, yet you remain confused;
- reconciliation with an estranged friend or mate, yet the gulf between you grows even wider;
- relief from crushing financial debt, yet the bills keep piling up; or
- supernatural healing for a loved one, yet he or she dies.

At these moments the Enemy slithers up to us and whispers in our ear this familiar taunt: "If God really cares for you, why didn't

He answer your request? Maybe He is not as powerful as you thought. Maybe He is angry with you. Maybe He doesn't care. Maybe He doesn't even really exist."

Frankly, any one of those claims—if true—is enough to quench our desire for more in our relationship with God. Who wants to pursue Him more intently if He doesn't love us, is not powerful enough to take care of us, doesn't care, or doesn't exist at all?

Unanswered prayer could give the Enemy a potentially powerful foothold in our lives...unless we remember some important truths.

Every Christian Wrestles with Unanswered Prayer

We are not alone if we feel abandoned by God. Noah felt abandoned when he spent more than a year on the ark without any word from the Almighty. Abraham felt abandoned when the Lord refused to fulfill His promise of a son for nearly twenty-five years. Hannah felt abandoned as she went to Shiloh year after year begging for a child. The apostle Paul felt abandoned as he pleaded with God for physical healing that never occurred. Jesus Himself felt abandoned as He hung on the cross and cried out, "My God, my God, why hast thou forsaken me?" (Matthew 27:46, KJV). We are not alone if we struggle with the disappointment of unanswered prayer. And yet we need to remember that God is at work even when we cannot see him working.

An inscription on a cellar wall in Germany where Jews hid from the Nazis reads:

> *I believe in the sun even when it is not shining.*
> *I believe in love even when feeling it not.*
> *I believe in God even when he is silent.*

I will never forget the night I heard that my mother, age fifty-six, had died. As I drove the back roads of West Texas late that night to our family home in Dallas, a thousand questions flooded my mind. "Lord, why would You take someone who was such an effective witness for You? Why didn't You answer our requests for healing? Why did You allow the doctors to misdiagnose her condition?"

Then I turned on the car radio and, almost immediately, heard these words spoken from Romans 11:33: "Oh, the depth of the riches both of the wisdom and knowledge of God! How unsearchable are His judgments and unfathomable His ways!" Within these few moments, God had supplied an answer to my desperate questions.

His wisdom is without limit.

His judgments are unsearchable.

His ways are unfathomable.

The phrase *ways of God* simply means "the workings of God"—in the world generally and in our lives specifically. Paul said that God's workings are "unfathomable." That word is a hunting term referring to the footprints of an animal that cannot be traced. God's workings in our lives are often difficult to track, especially ahead of time or when we are in the middle of a crisis.

For example, think about the Old Testament character Joseph. God had revealed to him as a teenager that one day he would be a great leader and would rule over his brothers. Yet his brothers sold him into slavery, later he was unjustly accused of rape, and finally, he was thrown into prison. In spite of his constant cries to God for deliverance, God remained silent and distant.

No doubt Joseph had a difficult time tracking God's "footprints" in his life during those two monotonous years in the dungeon. But unknown to Joseph, God was working in Pharaoh's life.

> Now it happened at the end of two full years that Pharaoh had a dream.… Then Pharaoh sent and called for Joseph, and they hurriedly brought him out of the dungeon. (Genesis 41:1,14)

On a day that began like any other day, Joseph awakened and heard footsteps approaching his cell. He heard the clanking of the soldier's keys. Suddenly the prison door flew open, and the sunlight flooded the darkness. Joseph's ordeal was over. God had said, "Enough."

And in time, God will say the same about *your* situation.

God does not operate according to our timetable, but according to His own. And in God's plan nothing is ever too long, too short, too early, or too late. As Ecclesiastes 3:11 assures us, God "has made everything appropriate in its time."

Lie No. 3: "God Has Cheated Me, Therefore I Must Disobey Him"

Satan is one of the most unoriginal creatures in the universe. You would think that after thousands of years of tempting individuals, he would come up with some new ideas. But he doesn't need to. Satan's methods have been so effective from the beginning of time, why change?

To gain some insight into Satan's strategy for destroying your life, it is helpful to go back and look at the very first instance recorded in the Bible of Satan's interaction with human beings. It is found in Genesis 3:

> Now the serpent was more crafty than any beast of the
> field which the LORD God had made. And he said to the
> woman, "Indeed, has God said, 'You shall not eat from any
> tree of the garden'?" (verse 1)

Most artistic representations of this story depict Eve dressed in designer fig leaves, listening intently to a snake wrapped around a branch as he speaks, quite literally, with a forked tongue. Ladies, how likely is it that you would carry on a conversation with a black, slimy snake that has slithered up next to you? Most women (and men) I know would run as quickly and as far as possible in the opposite direction.

Evil Disguised as Beauty

But the Bible tells us that it was not until after Adam and Eve's fall into sin that the serpent was transformed into the hideous creature we know today that crawls on its belly. Originally, Satan entered into what was probably the most beautiful creature in the world. And when Satan appears in your life, he will most likely follow a similar strategy, appearing as something you consider beautiful and desirable.

The other night I was talking to my teenage daughter about her favorite topic: boys. Actually, I was the one doing the talking while she rolled her eyes. But I reminded her that one way Satan would try to destroy her life would be to bring the wrong boy into her life. And that boy would not be a pimple-faced wimp wearing thick glasses. He would probably be the most popular, good-looking (or "hot," as they say) boy in the school.

And this principle holds true for every one of us. When Satan comes into your life, don't expect a red-flanneled, long-tailed creature with two horns and a pitchfork. He is much too clever for that. I love the way my former seminary professor Haddon Robinson describes Satan's preferred appearance:

> When Satan comes to you, he does not come in the form of a coiled snake. He does not approach with the roar of a lion. He does not come with the wail of a siren. He does not come waving a red flag. Satan simply slides into your life. When he appears, he seems almost like a comfortable companion. There's nothing about him that you would dread.[9]

QUESTIONING GOD'S RELIABILITY

As Satan sidled up next to Eve, he asked her the first recorded question in the Bible. "Has God said...?" The first words from the Enemy's mouth questioned the reliability of the Word of God: "Eve, how do you know that God *really* said this? Since God did not speak to you directly, how do you know that God really spoke to Adam? And if He did speak to Adam, how do you know that Adam heard the message correctly and reported it to you accurately?"

Satan continues to attack the veracity of God's Word in the very same way today. If he can ever cause you to question the truthfulness of the Bible, your ultimate rebellion against God becomes a piece of cake to him.

Recently I spoke at the funeral service of my father in the ministry, Dr. W. A. Criswell, pastor of the historic First Baptist Church in Dallas. In my tribute, I recounted a turbulent time in my life when, as a college student, I listened to professors point out the alleged inconsistencies and contradictions in the Bible. A steady diet of that kind of instruction led many of my classmates to abandon their faith. But Dr. Criswell's faithful proclamation that *every word of the Bible was God-breathed* kept me grounded in the faith. For that I will be forever grateful to him.

Interestingly (and purposefully), Satan misquoted God's instruction. The Lord did not command the first couple to refrain from eating from "any tree of the garden." In fact, God told them that *every* tree was created for their enjoyment *except one*. Yet Satan twisted God's command, which emphasized His abundant provision ("any tree of the garden") and instead focused on God's one prohibition ("you shall not eat").

Do you notice how he uses the same tactic today? Listen to the media try to describe the Christian's view of sexuality, and they will imply that all Christians believe sex is a dirty, shameful activity to be avoided at all cost. The unbeliever then asks, "Why would God create us with sexual drives if He did not intend for us to satisfy those desires?" But has God said sex is wrong? Of course not! He's the One who thought up the idea! God has invited us to enjoy our sexuality with just one restriction. Sex is exclusively reserved for the marriage relationship. But Satan loves to focus on God's limited prohibition instead of on His limitless provisions—which leads to Satan's next strategy.

QUESTIONING GOD'S GOODNESS

If Satan cannot persuade us to question the Word of God, then he will cause us to question the goodness of God. To Eve's credit, she corrected Satan's misquotation of God's command. But Satan was not through with her. He promised her that if she did disobey God's command, "You surely will not die! For God knows that in the day you eat from it your eyes will be opened, and you will be like God, knowing good and evil" (Genesis 3:4-5).

The Enemy was saying, in effect, "God does not have your best interest at heart. He is paranoid, fearing that if you eat from the tree you will become just like Him—and God can't handle the competition."

Ultimately, the basis for every temptation we encounter is the question, "Is God's way really best for me? Is God looking out for His interests or my interests? Is God trying to make me happy or miserable?" In his book *The Serpent of Paradise,* Erwin Lutzer asks:

> Why are we so often lured by temptation? Because we have been conned by the idea that God's way for us is not best. We believe that our obedience might be best for Him, but not for us. But Luther was right when he said that "all sin is contempt of God."[10]

Can you trust God? Do you believe that His commands about sex, honesty, marriage, or obedience to authority are given for your benefit as well as for His glory?

Eve's belief in the truthfulness of God's Word remained intact. What ultimately caused her to succumb to Satan's temptation was her lack of faith in the goodness of God. Tragically, Eve bought into the lie that God was trying to cheat her out of true happiness in life. And the rest, as they say, is history.

CONFIDENCE IN GOD'S CHARACTER

"God has condemned me."

"God has abandoned me."

"God has cheated me."

Will you notice that each one of Satan's lies is really an indictment of God's character? Satan will continually try to persuade you to question God's forgiveness, God's care, or God's wisdom in your life.

How do we defend against such attacks? If indeed every one of Satan's assaults is based on a lie designed to cause you to question God's character, may I encourage you to read, meditate, perhaps even memorize a section of Scripture that reminds us of God's *real* attitude toward His children? I can't think of a passage of Scripture that accomplishes that better than Ephesians 1:3-8:

> How we praise God, the Father of our Lord Jesus Christ, who has blessed us with every spiritual blessing in the heavenly realms because we belong to Christ. Long ago, even before he made the world, God loved us and chose us in Christ to be holy and without fault in his eyes. His unchanging plan has always been to adopt us into his own family by bringing us to himself though Jesus Christ. And

this gave him great pleasure. So we praise God for the wonderful kindness he has poured out on us because we belong to his dearly loved Son. He is so rich in kindness that he purchased our freedom through the blood of his Son, and our sins are forgiven. He has showered his kindness on us, along with all wisdom and understanding. (NLT)

Think of all God has done for you. He chose you…before you ever chose Him. He decided to adopt you into His family while you were still His enemy. He redeemed you from the marketplace of sin when Satan still had you in his grip. He forgave you of *all* your sins without asking you for anything. And He has showered you with His kindness…for no other reason than the fact that He decided to love *you*.

Don't you think that such a God is worthy of our trust, even when we don't always understand what He is up to in our lives?

Many of you are familiar with noted speaker and author Elisabeth Elliot. As a young girl she married Jim Elliot, and together they worked with the Auca Indians in Ecuador. Jim and Elisabeth had been married only twenty-seven months when he and four other missionaries were speared to death by the Aucas. But that was not the end. Some years later, Elisabeth married another committed Christian man who died a slow and painful death.

What is Elisabeth Elliot's conclusion about the "ways of God" in her life? Instead of offering the sugar-coated Sunday-school answer you might expect, she is refreshingly honest:

The experiences of my life are not such that I could infer from them that God is good, gracious and merciful necessarily. To have one husband murdered and another one disintegrate body, soul and spirit, through cancer, is not what you would call a proof of the love of God. In fact, there are many times when it looks like just the opposite. But my belief in the love of God is not by inference or instinct. It is by faith. To apprehend God's sovereignty working in that love is—we must say it—the last and highest victory of the faith that overcomes the world.[11]

It is that kind of faith in the power, wisdom, and goodness of God that ultimately overcomes the attacks of Satan against those who are searching for more.

Ten

SATISFIED FOREVER!

Being a Special-K Christian in a Krispy-Kreme World

In his book *The Life God Blesses,* Gordon MacDonald described two very different breakfast regimens in his household. His wife chooses fruit, while he fills his breakfast bowl with a popular cereal high on flavor (and sugar), but low on nutrition. When he finishes draining the bowl of its contents, he feels terrific and bounds out of the house ready to face the day. However, after a few hours he finds himself hungry and wondering when lunch will arrive. Why?

> My enjoyable breakfast cereal with its sugar has done little
> to give me enduring strength for the day. It has offered only
> the perception of a satisfying breakfast, but the promise is
> short-lived. Sugar has let me down with a thud within a
> short time....
> Gail's fruit carries her throughout the morning, and she
> never forgets to tell me this....
> Gail has opted for nutrition; I have chosen taste.[1]

Every person faces his own temptations. While Gordon's sugar-coated cereal has never held much sway over me, I encountered my own breakfast temptress this week. Our local supermarket has just started carrying those deliciously sinful Krispy Kreme donuts. The supermarket manager wisely places boxes of those doughnuts at the entrance of the store so I must confront them every time I walk through the doors. Although I know I should head straight for the cereal aisle and pick up a box of Special K, the siren song of the Krispy Kremes can be overpowering.

While the players in my temptation are different, the choice is the same. Taste or nutrition? Happiness or health? Short-term exhilaration or long-term satisfaction?

The dilemma of taste versus nutrition is not limited to the world of breakfast foods. Ultimately, we must choose the kind of spiritual diet we are going to pursue as we search for more in our relationship with God. We must decide between sugar or substance, short-term fixes or long-term solutions, exhilaration or transformation. In short, we must decide whether we want to be a Krispy-Kreme or a Special-K kind of Christian.

As we saw in the first chapter, many Christians have a holy hunger for "more" in their relationship with God. They genuinely desire to experience the supernatural power and presence of God in their lives. There is absolutely nothing wrong—and everything right—with such a desire. But the question is, "How do I satisfy my hunger for more?"

The Krispy-Kreme Christian is the one who attempts to satisfy that spiritual hunger with quick fixes rather than long-term solutions. He or she is always searching after new experiences such as fresh revelations from God, miraculous manifestations of God's power, and immediate (and satisfactory) answers to prayer. In short, the Krispy-Kreme Christian is looking for experiences rather than spirituality. Gordon MacDonald describes four characteristics of spiritual experiences that always leave us empty and hungering for more:

1. Spiritual experiences require little discipline. Since experiences by and large are dependent on external forces such as music, preaching, or supernatural manifestations, the participant need not engage in such mundane and laborious disciplines as reading the Bible, praying, worshiping, or obeying.

2. Spiritual experiences focus more on emotion than on change. After the shouting stops, the tears dry, or the goose bumps subside, the participant remains the way he was before the experience.

3. Spiritual experiences are short-lived. Like the sugar-induced high, the spiritual experience is great while it lasts, but the problem is that it doesn't last long enough. After the experience passes, the participant finds himself depressed and craving another—and usually more intense—experience to induce the same level of exhilaration.

4. Spiritual experiences usually focus on the participant rather than on God. Whenever we—or even the Holy Spirit—become the focus of our spiritual experience, we have missed the point completely.[2]

TO ILLUMINATE JESUS CHRIST

The purpose of the Holy Spirit's supernatural power in our lives is not to bring attention to ourselves or even to Himself, but to our Lord Jesus Christ. Jesus explained the primary purpose of the Holy Spirit this way: "He [the Holy Spirit] will glorify Me" (John 16:14).

J. I. Packer compares the Holy Spirit to a floodlight. The purpose of a floodlight is to bring attention to a designated object without calling attention to itself. My father used to work for an airline, so as a youngster, I spent a lot of time around airports and airplanes. I remember seeing the tails of large jetliners with their famous red TWA logo brightly illuminated at night. No light fixtures were visible on the jets' tails, so for years I tried to figure out the source of that light. Finally someone explained that the floodlight was recessed into the bottom portion of the tail section so that it would be hidden from view and would not create unnecessary drag on the airplane.

In the same way, the Holy Spirit is deeply recessed into our lives. His purpose for residing in us is not to draw attention to us or even to Himself, but to illuminate Jesus Christ. As Packer says:

> The Spirit's message to us is never, "Look at me; listen to me; come to me; get to know me," but always, "Look at *him* [Jesus Christ], and see his glory; listen to *him,* and hear his word; go to *him,* and have life; get to know *him,* and taste his gift of joy and peace."[3]

TRUE SPIRITUALITY: THE SATISFIED SOUL

"All right, Robert, you've explained that the Krispy-Kreme Christian chooses experiences over true spirituality. But what do you mean by 'true spirituality'?" Supreme Court Justice Potter Stewart was once asked to define pornography. He replied, "I can't define it, but I know it when I see it." Likewise, spirituality is hard to define, but we know true spirituality when we see it.

The most effective way to define true spirituality is not by explanation, but by illustration. One of our best examples of a Special-K kind of believer is the Old Testament patriarch Abraham. Here is a person who knew all about genuine and lasting satisfaction. He had a holy hunger for "more" in his relationship with God that was ultimately fulfilled. Look at how Abraham finished his life: "Abraham breathed his last and died in a ripe old age, an old man and *satisfied* with life" (Genesis 25:8).

My ministerial profession requires me to spend a lot of time in cemeteries, but I don't recall ever seeing a tombstone etched with the words "Satisfied with Life." Yet can you think of a better epitaph? Isn't that what we all long for? Wouldn't you like your last breath to be a sigh of contentment rather than a groan of disappointment?

What was it about Abraham's life that produced this deep feeling of satisfaction? Certainly, we could choose a number of memorable snapshots from his life to illustrate his commitment to God that resulted in his contentment: his departure from his home country in obedience to God; his belief in God's promise of a great nation; his intercession for the cities of Sodom and Gomorrah; and perhaps the signal event in his life, the offering of his son, Isaac, as a sacrifice to God.

But I want to point to an early episode in Abraham's life that, I believe, illustrates even more vividly what we mean by true spirituality…and explains the source of Abraham's deep sense of satisfaction. The event was a simple real estate transaction with a relative, but the choices Abraham made are the same choices that confront every Christian who truly wants more in his relationship with God.

> So Abram went up from Egypt to the Negev, he and his wife
> and all that belonged to him; and Lot with him.… And the
> land could not sustain them while dwelling together, for
> their possessions were so great that they were not able to
> remain together. And there was strife between the herdsmen
> of Abram's livestock and the herdsmen of Lot's livestock.…
> So Abram said to Lot, "Please let there be no strife between
> you and me, nor between my herdsmen and your herdsmen,
> for we are brothers. Is not the whole land before you? Please

separate from me; if to the left, then I will go to the right; or
if to the right, then I will go to the left." Lot lifted up his
eyes and saw all the valley of the Jordan, that it was well
watered everywhere.... So Lot chose for himself all the valley
of the Jordan.... Abram settled in the land of Canaan, while
Lot settled in the cities of the valley, and moved his tents as
far as Sodom. (Genesis 13:1,6-12)

After a brief stint in Egypt, Abraham and his family (including
his nephew Lot) returned to the Promised Land. Their family fortune, measured in livestock in those days, had grown so dramatically that the family faced a problem. It is interesting to note that
this passage marks the first time the term *wealth* is used in the
Bible, and it is used in a negative sense. While there is certainly
nothing wrong with money, it usually brings its own special conflicts. For example, a husband and wife who have struggled together for decades finally achieve prosperity—and then decide to
divorce and go their separate ways. The division of assets is often
the cause of much bickering and legal maneuvering. Even churches
are not exempt from conflicts over wealth: A number of pastors
have told me that the biggest fights they have seen in their churches
were not over financial shortfalls, but over how to spend financial
surpluses.

In Abraham's case, the cause of the conflict was that the land
was incapable of supporting both his and Lot's increasing herds of
livestock. So Abraham made a proposal: "Lot, we need to spread
out. You choose whatever land you want, and I'll take what is left."
Even though he was the patriarch of the family, Abraham willingly
surrendered his rights in deference to Lot.

What caused him to make such a choice?

He was a Special-K kind of believer, more interested in long-
term satisfaction than in short-term gain. To help us better under-

stand the concept of true spirituality, allow me to identify three "ingredients" of the Special-K believer (Abraham) in contrast to the Krispy-Kreme variety (Lot).

A GREATER PURPOSE

Every life is either self-focused or God-focused. It's one or the other; it can't be both. Jesus said, "No one can serve two masters" (Matthew 6:24). A friend of mine said it this way: "Every life exists either to meet a need or to fill a greed."

Lot's focus was the latter.

His philosophy of life is still prevalent today: "Get all you can, can all you get, and sit on the can." Lot already possessed plenty of wealth. His choice was not based on need, but on greed. The text says that Lot "saw all the valley of the Jordan, that it was well watered everywhere." The word translated *saw* carries the idea of "gazing with a longing." As Lot looked longingly at the plush green land of the Jordan valley, he thought to himself, *If only I had* that *piece of real estate,* then *I could be truly satisfied.*

Do you know what the greatest enemy of satisfaction in life is? It is what I call "the oasis syndrome." It is believing that happiness in life is somewhere other than where I am at the present. If only...

I had that job;

I had that mate;

I had that amount of money;

I had that spiritual experience; *then*

I would be truly happy.

I was once interviewed by a well-known figure whose last name is synonymous with positive thinking. I was discussing this whole idea of the oasis syndrome and how it wars against content-ment in life. Finally, the host couldn't take it any longer and blurted out, "What's wrong with looking for an oasis? Our toll-free number is 1-800-OASIS!"

Here's what's wrong with an oasis: It will *always* outdistance you. Every time. Once you get there, it is never what you imagined it to be. And there will always be another oasis just beyond your reach.

In contrast to Lot, Abraham had a greater purpose in life than his own immediate satisfaction. First, he was concerned about the well-being of his entire family. His plea for unity ("Please let there be no strife between you and me") was based on the realization that the Canaanites living in the land were ready to pounce at the first sign of division between the two. Abraham understood the principle, "United we stand, divided we fall," and was committed to keeping peace in the family—even if that peace meant surrendering some of his own rights.

By the way, we would do well to remember this in the church. We have a commitment to the well-being of one another because we are all part of God's family. One of my pet peeves is talking to visitors to our church who say, "We enjoyed the visit, but we are just shopping around." In other words, "Our commitment to a church is going to be based on what you can do for us." And even if they happen to join, their commitment is good only until something "better" comes along, or until they disagree with a decision that is made, or until they get their feelings hurt over some real or imagined slight. What a far cry that is from the kind of commitment Paul called for in Romans 12:10: "Be devoted to one another in brotherly love; give preference to one another in honor."

The word translated *devoted* refers to the natural affection that siblings should have for one another, since they are "from the same womb" (the literal meaning of the word translated *brotherly*). Unfortunately, such concern is missing in many families and in many churches. Instead, the typical church resembles a mother pig surrounded by her little piglets that are desperately trying to get at the milk their mother offers. They squeal, they push, they prod, and they do whatever is necessary to get their turn at the teat. Why? They have one thing on their mind: immediate gratification, with no thought for their brother and sister piglets.

Many Christians view the church as one giant—(do I dare even say it?). They believe the church exists for one reason—to satisfy *their* needs. And woe to anyone who gets in their way. Stuart Briscoe writes: "More often than not trouble erupts in the fellowship because people are offended when they perceive, rightly or wrongly, that their positions have been usurped or their personhood has been slighted. The insistence on position and rights rather than privilege and responsibility is the seedbed in which a variegated crop of evil flourishes."

Just as God places every one of us into a family when we are born, He desires that each of us be part of a family of believers when we are born again. The reason God places us into both physical and spiritual families is not only to receive the nurturing we need, but also to develop the character God desires. Living in any kind of family forces us to be confronted with other needs besides our own.

But Abraham's greater purpose extended beyond a concern for his family's well-being. Ultimately, Abraham was focused on the plan and program of God. If the Canaanites in the land had been able to gain victory over Abraham because of an internal family struggle, then God's reputation for protecting His people would have been severely damaged. For the Special-K believer, God's reputation and purpose always trump the believer's individual preferences and immediate comfort.

A GREATER FAITH

Lot probably thought his old uncle Abraham was showing signs of senility to have allowed him to choose the better piece of land. Abraham would never have made such an offer in his younger days. (You don't get to be a Middle Eastern tycoon like Abraham by being Mr. Nice Guy.)

But through an earlier episode in his life, Abraham had learned the hard way about the danger of believing that you are responsible for your own well-being. After arriving in the Promised Land, Abraham and company had been immediately faced with a problem: "Now there was a famine in the land" (Genesis 12:10).

Abraham had just received God's sweeping promise of a land that would be his forever; of a nation whose citizenry would be innumerable; and of a blessing that would extend through him to all the nations of the world. But Abraham faced a potential disaster that would nullify all of those promises. The rains that usually came in the latter part of the year had failed to materialize. *Can I trust God to meet my needs?* he asked himself. *Although God miraculously brought me to this place, can He be depended upon to provide for me and for my family?*

Does this sound familiar to you? Perhaps God has supernaturally uprooted you and brought you to a new job, a new city, a new church, or a new family situation. But now you are facing an unexpected crisis, and you are wondering if the same God who brought you to this place can be counted on to sustain you.

Tragically, Abraham concluded that God was incapable of taking care of him and his family. With no end to the famine in sight, he packed up his family and left for Egypt.

Please understand that Abraham's motive was absolutely pure: He was trying to provide for his family. He surveyed his situation and saw there was need. He correctly concluded that the Canaanites living in the land would be of no help. There is nothing wrong with using logic in problem solving. But…as thoroughly as he may have thought the situation through, *he left God out of the equation.* Not once did Abraham ask God for guidance or for supernatural intervention. Instead, he concluded that "If it's going to be, it's up to me."

Mark it down: Any time you leave God out of the mix, you are going to make a bad decision. Abraham certainly did. His decision to uproot his family and move to Egypt ended in disaster and disgrace.

So when we come to the story of Abraham and Lot in Genesis 13, Abraham has just returned from Egypt dragging his tail between his legs. He has learned his lesson well. As long as he places God's interests above his own, he doesn't have to worry about his survival. Because Abraham has dedicated himself to a higher purpose in life—his family's well-being and God's eternal glory—he happily defers to Lot.

What if Lot gets the best of him and Abraham ends up with a patch of real estate unable to support him and his family? No problem. "God, if my family starves to death, You're the One who is going to look bad. You're the One who promised to make me the father of a great nation. Do You want unbelievers to say, 'God can't even take care of His own people?' This is Your responsibility, deal with it."

I have concluded that the source of all worry is assuming responsibility that God never intended for us to shoulder. For example: Parents, God has given you the responsibility for training your children, but ultimately you are not responsible for their choices in life. If you do assume responsibility for those choices, your life will be filled with anxiety.

Maybe you are a single adult looking for a mate. While God has given you certain guidelines for choosing a husband or wife, finding that marriage partner is God's responsibility, not yours. Taking that responsibility upon yourself will only produce unbearable stress.

And pastors, God has given you the charge to faithfully teach the Word of God, but He assumes responsibility for growing the church. Jesus said, "*I* will build My church," not "*We* will build My church." Relax and allow God to bear the responsibility that He says belongs to Him. (That sure sounds good to me; I write these words on a Monday morning after a disappointing Sunday.)

The foundation of the Special-K believer's life is faith, and the essence of faith is believing that God will do what He has promised to do.

An Eternal Horizon

Investment advisors tells us that the longer the amount of time before you retire, the greater the risks you can afford to take in your investment program. For example, if you are going to need your money in a year, then you had better place your money in a low-risk investment such as a CD or money market fund. The returns are paltry, but the principal is secure. However, if you have twenty years before you retire, you can afford to take greater risks in search of greater reward. Although in any given year you may suffer a temporary loss, over the long term those losses are likely to be more than compensated by greater returns. You have to understand your "investment horizon," as advisors say.

The reason Abraham was willing to take a risk in offering Lot the better land is that Abraham had a longer investment horizon than Lot. Even if he suffered a temporary loss because of Lot's greed, Abraham was confident that, in the long term, God would reward him for his faithfulness. The writer of Hebrews described Abraham's perspective this way: "He was looking for the city which has foundations, whose architect and builder is God" (Hebrews 11:10).

Abraham's investment horizon was not limited to one month, one year, one decade, or even one lifetime. His investment horizon was eternity. And because of that, Abraham was willing to place God's eternal glory above his own temporary satisfaction. In fact, Abraham's eternal mind-set is the only explanation for just about every significant decision in his life. Why else would Abraham choose to

- believe he could be the father of a great nation when all the evidence was to the contrary?
- leave everything and everyone familiar to him in quest of an unfamiliar country?
- offer his long-awaited child of promise as a human sacrifice to God?

Abraham had a longer investment horizon. He believed that over time—a long period of time—God would reward him for his obedience. Interestingly, Abraham (as well as the other heroes of the faith described in Hebrews 11) died without receiving that reward they had been promised.

> All these died in faith, without receiving the promises, but having seen them and having welcomed them from a distance, and having confessed that they were strangers and exiles on the earth.... But as it is, they desire a better country, that is, a heavenly one. (verses 13,16)

Although he died without receiving the reward he had anticipated, Abraham still died "satisfied with life." Why? Because he had an eternal investment horizon. He was looking for a greater reward, even if that reward was waiting for him on the other side of the grave.

And I believe that is the most distinguishing difference between the Krispy-Kreme and the Special-K believer. The former will attempt to satisfy the desire for "more" in his or her relationship with God with experiences that produce short-term exhilaration but, in the long run, leave them empty and discontent. The Special-K believer, on the other hand, understands that "mundane" disciplines such as Bible study, prayer, involvement in a

church, and obedience to God *may* not bring immediate gratification…but over the long term will pave the way for the Holy Spirit's
supernatural work in his or her life.

It Really Isn't About *Us*

About a year ago a woman in our church—a thirty-seven-year-old
mother of two young boys—was diagnosed with a rare form of
incurable cancer. Carole and her husband, Ken, sought the best
medical advice available. Yet they knew that, ultimately, her healing would have to come from God. Ken came from a denomination that emphasized miraculous healings, and he listened to a
series of tapes by a well-known proponent of faith healing. He was
convinced that his wife's deliverance from this illness was God's
will. One day he asked that I and some of the leaders of the church
lay hands on his wife and pray for healing, which we gladly did.

The last year has been an emotional roller coaster for the couple
and their two young sons. The doctors told them that Carole's cancer had spread to the pancreas. This, of course, devastated them.
Then the doctors said they had made a mistake; there was no cancer in the pancreas. So we thanked God for what appeared to be a
miraculous healing. But then the doctors said they had misread the
tests and that the cancer indeed *was* in the pancreas. It has been a
traumatic, exhausting year of ups and downs for this dear family.

Last Monday evening I stopped at hospice to see Carole and
Ken. If I live to be one hundred, I will never forget what Ken said
to me as he held the hand of his beloved wife as she was about to
slip into eternity. "Pastor, I hate the cancer. But I love what the cancer has done for our family and for our faith. It has drawn us closer
to one another and closer to God."

Only a person with an eternal horizon could make such a statement. A year of unanswered prayers and unanswered questions had

led him to the conclusion that God is much more interested in what happens *in* us than in what happens *to* us. Our financial condition, our relationships, and our health can change in an instant. But the Holy Spirit's supernatural work of molding us into the image of Christ endures for eternity. The person with the long-term horizon understands that it really isn't about us—it is about Him in us.

That realization is the starting point for anyone truly searching for more.

STUDY AND DISCUSSION GUIDE

CHAPTER 1: A HOLY HUNGER

1. What motivated you to purchase this book? Could you identify with one of the three scenarios described at the beginning of the chapter? Which one and why?

2. Do you agree with the premise that most Christians are not really experiencing the supernatural power of the Holy Spirit in their lives? Why or why not?

3. Review the questions on pages 10-11. As you reflect on your answers, how would you summarize the state of your relationship with God right now? If that relationship is not as "hot" as it once was, why do you think it has changed?

4. Do you agree that there is little behavioral difference between most Christians and non-Christians? If so, describe some areas in which Christians should be noticeably different but perhaps are not. How do you explain this lack of personal victory—what the author calls "the disconnect between belief and behavior"?

5. When you are faced with a crisis, what is your first response? Why do you think people do not pray more for God's supernatural intervention in their crises?

6. Do you believe that God continues to perform miracles today in the same way He did in biblical times? Why or why not?

7. In a few sentences, complete this thought: "As a result of reading this book, I am praying that my relationship with God will be…"

CHAPTER 2: YOU'RE RICHER THAN YOU THINK!

1. Identify one or two things you learned about the Holy Spirit that you did not know before reading this chapter.
2. How does the fact that the Holy Spirit is a Person, rather than an object, affect your attitude toward Him?
3. Should Christians pray for the Holy Spirit to come into their lives? Why or why not?
4. How would you explain to a new Christian the "baptism with the Holy Spirit"?
5. If it is true that "by nature" no one is hungry for God and no one seeks after God (see Romans 3:10-11), apart from the supernatural work of the Holy Spirit, how do you explain many unbelievers' interest in spiritual issues?
6. Have you discovered your spiritual gift? If so, what difference has the knowledge of your gift made in your life and in those around you?
7. A friend says, "I don't think you can ever know for sure if you are going to heaven until you die." How would you respond? What role does the Holy Spirit play in the assurance of our salvation?

CHAPTER 3: THE SECOND BLESSING

1. Beyond the time you trusted Christ as your Savior, what is the most significant spiritual experience in your life? What do you think precipitated this experience?
2. Summarize the difference between the "baptism with the Holy Spirit" and the "filling of the Holy Spirit."
3. After reading this chapter, do you believe that every Christian is permanently *indwelt* by the Holy Spirit? Why or why not?
4. Why do you think there is such confusion today over the baptism with the Holy Spirit?

5. How would you respond to a friend who said, "I am addicted to _____ (pornography, alcohol, drugs, etc.). Although I am a Christian and have prayed for deliverance from this addiction, God is not answering my prayers. Why doesn't the Holy Spirit give me the power to overcome this addiction?"

6. As Christians, do we have to sin? Theoretically, would it be possible for a Christian to completely abstain from sin? Why or why not? How do you reconcile your answer with the truth of the "new nature" the author explains in this chapter?

7. Describe a time in your life when you have felt the Holy Spirit taking control of your life. What do you think prevents that from happening more often?

CHAPTER 4: WHAT GOD DESIRES FROM YOU

1. Have you ever been the victim of "upward delegation"? How did it make you feel? What did you do to prevent it from happening again?

2. Think about a painful experience in your life. How does Romans 8:28-29 apply to that experience? What new insights did you gain from the author's explanation of "God causes all things to work together for good" that will be helpful to you in the future?

3. Reflect on the explanation of "sanctification" in this chapter. Do you agree with the author's premise that "sanctification is a cooperative effort between God and us"? Why or why not?

4. Toward which of the two extreme views of sanctification do you tend to gravitate: passivity or self-reliance? What has been the result?

5. What motivates some Christians to take the passive view of the Christian life? What motivates others to be self-reliant?

6. Do you think it is possible for us to do something that guarantees the release of God's supernatural power in our lives? If so, what? If not, why not?

7. If God were to sit down with you and evaluate your relationship with Him, what things would He commend you for? What areas would He say needed some work?

CHAPTER 5: HOW TO TAKE A SPIRITUAL BATH

1. Does your church place a proper emphasis on the Bible? Cite some evidence to support your answer.

2. Do you agree that many conservative churches that profess a belief in the inspiration of the Scriptures have turned away from solid, biblical instruction? If so, why do you think that is?

3. Go back and review the four questions on page 84. If you find it difficult to make reading and studying the Bible a priority in your life, why do you think it has been a challenge for you? What practical step(s) are you willing to take, starting this week, to make personal Bible study a top priority?

4. Can you recall an incident in your life in which the Bible gave you specific guidance and/or assurance about a decision you faced?

5. The author says that God uses His Word to bring spiritual healing in our lives. Does this mean that Christians should not rely on counselors or books apart from the Bible for help? Why or why not?

6. Do you believe God speaks to Christians apart from the Bible today? Explain and defend your answer.

7. What one specific change do you plan to make in your life as a result of reading this chapter?

Chapter 6: The Power of Faith Kneeling

1. Have you ever experienced "prayer fade" in your life? If so, what do you think caused you to slip into prayer-fade mode?
2. How would you respond to the question, "Why pray if God is going to do what He wants to do anyway?"
3. If prayer is one of the main conduits through which the power of God flows into our lives, why don't we pray more? Why is prayer such hard work?
4. A friend asks you, "Is it wrong for me to pray that I will get the job promotion I really want?" How would you answer? How do you reconcile Matthew 7:7-11, in which Jesus encourages us to ask God for anything, and James 4:3, which warns against asking with selfish motives?
5. Why should we ask God to "forgive us our debts" if we have already been forgiven of our sins when we trusted in Christ as our Savior?
6. Have you ever struggled with unanswered prayer? What did you learn about God and yourself as a result of that struggle?
7. Which of the author's suggestions for becoming a more effective "pray-er" make the most sense to you? If this chapter has changed your attitude or insight about prayer, describe what has changed your perspective.

Chapter 7: Up with Worship!

1. Have you ever questioned the importance of being part of a church? Why or why not?
2. Why do you think so many Christians view the church negatively?
3. Reread Ephesians 5:25-27. Describe one or two insights about the church you have gained from reading this passage and chapter 7 of this book.

4. If you were in the same situation as Rick and Sharon Ballew (the couple mentioned in the opening pages of this chapter), which church would you have chosen? Why?

5. Imagine that your child is about to leave home for college. You explain to him or her the importance of joining a church, and your child asks, "Why do I need to join a church?" How would you answer that question?

6. Review the four functions of the church—winning, instruction, nourishment, and sharing. Do you believe one function is more important than the others, or do you feel all four should be in balance? To what function do you feel God has called (or *is calling*) you to lend your time and talent? If you are not currently involved in helping your church's ministry, will you ask God to clearly lead you to assist with at least one of the four functions of your church?

7. If Jesus Christ were evaluating your church, what things would He commend your church for? Which areas would He say need improvement?

CHAPTER 8: FLAMETHROWERS VS. FIRE EXTINGUISHERS

1. What does it mean to "quench" the work of the Holy Spirit? As you reflect on your own experience, what types of things have you done in the past that have quenched the working of God's Spirit in your life?

2. Do you agree with the author that sexual immorality is different from other sins? Why or why not? (See 1 Corinthians 6:18-19.)

3. Why do you think Christians struggle so much with sins of sexual immorality?

4. In Matthew 6:15, Jesus warned, "But if you do not forgive others, then your Father will not forgive your transgressions."

Does this verse mean that those who refuse to forgive others cannot be forgiven by God? Why or why not?

5. What do you think makes it difficult for us to forgive other people? What are we to do even if the transgressor is not sorry or repentant?

6. Why do you believe there are so many commands in the Bible to "fear not"? If someone were to ask you for some practical ways to overcome worry, what advice would you offer?

7. At the close of the chapter, the author encourages you to identify "one thing" that may be quenching the Holy Spirit's power in your life. Do you know what that "one thing" is? List two specific steps you can take this week to begin eliminating that barrier to experiencing more of God's power in your life.

CHAPTER 9: BATTLE READY!

1. "We need to hear more sermons and read more books that teach us about the reality and work of Satan." Do you agree or disagree with that statement? Why?

2. Read Luke 8:26-39, which recounts Jesus' experience with a man possessed by demons. What does this story reveal to you about Satan and his demonic forces?

3. Why do you think many Christians are unaware of the spiritual struggle in which they are engaged?

4. As you reflect on your life, is there some past sin that Satan still uses to hinder your relationship with God? What specific insights did you gain from this chapter to help you overcome guilt?

5. Have you ever felt abandoned by God? What event precipitated that feeling? How were you able to overcome your feeling of distance from God?

6. Why do you think it so difficult at times for us to see the "ways" or workings of God in our lives? Describe a personal experience in which you may have had difficulty trusting God's sovereignty, but in hindsight, you can now see His purpose in it all.

7. What makes sin so appealing to us? What one insight have you gained from this chapter to help correct wrong thinking that results in disobedience to God?

CHAPTER 10: SATISFIED FOREVER!

1. Why do you think so many people gravitate toward spiritual experiences rather than true spirituality?

2. Honestly evaluate your church. Does your church encourage Christians to pursue spiritual experiences or spirituality? If the former is true, what could you do to help change that?

3. If you were to die right now, could you honestly have Abraham's epitaph ("He died satisfied with life") placed on your tombstone? Why or why not?

4. Do you think most Christians have a clear sense of purpose in their lives? Why or why not? If you were to summarize your life purpose, what would it be?

5. Recently, two lesbians who claimed to be Christians appeared on a national television program. When challenged about their lifestyle, one of them responded, "If God is unhappy with me, why is He blessing me in so many ways?" How would you answer that question? Why doesn't God immediately punish or reward our behavior?

6. How do you define faith? What are you trusting God to do for (and *in*) you, even though you may be having difficulty seeing His hand at work?

7. As you come to the close of this book, what is the most valu-
    able truth you have discovered (or had reaffirmed) about
    your relationship with God? Identify one or two changes are
    you ready to make in your life as a result of reading *I Want
    More!*

NOTES

CHAPTER 1

1. Jim Cymbala, *Fresh Wind, Fresh Fire* (Grand Rapids: Zondervan, 1997), 55.

2. Charles R. Swindoll, *Flying Closer to the Flame* (Dallas: Word, 1993), 26-7.

CHAPTER 2

1. A. W. Tozer, quoted in Gordon MacDonald, *The Life God Blesses* (Nashville: Nelson, 1994), 205.

2. Philip Yancey, *Reaching for the Invisible God* (Grand Rapids: Zondervan, 2000), 149.

3. Merrill Unger, quoted in John F. MacArthur Jr., *The Charismatics* (Grand Rapids: Zondervan, 1978), 94.

4. For a more detailed discussion of these passages see chapter 8, "The Issue of Historical Transition," in MacArthur's *The Charismatics*.

5. James Montgomery Boice, *Romans,* vol. 1 (Grand Rapids: Baker, 1991), 302.

6. Ray Stedman, quoted in James Montgomery Boice, *Romans,* vol. 4 (Grand Rapids: Baker, 1995), 1569.

7. Max Anders, *The Good Life* (Dallas: Word, 1993), 42.

8. Billy Graham, quoted in Charles Stanley, *The Wonderful Spirit-Filled Life* (Nashville: Nelson, 1992), 39.

CHAPTER 3

1. D. L. Moody, quoted in Gordon MacDonald, *The Life God Blesses* (Nashville: Nelson, 1994), 206-7.

2. R. A. Torrey, quoted in Charles Stanley, *The Wonderful Spirit-Filled Life* (Nashville: Nelson, 1992), 34.

3. Vance Havner, in Jerry Vines, *Spirit Life* (Nashville: Broadman & Holman, 1998), 64.

4. Dwight Edwards, *Revolution Within* (Colorado Springs: WaterBrook, 2001), 5.

5. John Stott, in James Montgomery Boice, *Romans,* vol. 2 (Grand Rapids: Baker, 1992), 655.

CHAPTER 4

1. J. I. Packer, *Keep in Step with the Spirit* (Old Tappan, N.J.: Revell, 1984), 257.

CHAPTER 5

1. Erwin W. Lutzer, *Seven Reasons Why You Can Trust the Bible* (Chicago: Moody, 1998), 193.

2. Donald N. Bastian, "The Silenced Word," *Christianity Today* 45, no. 4 (5 March 2001): 1 (online edition).

3. Gary M. Burge, "The Greatest Story Never Read," *Christianity Today* 43, no. 9 (9 August 1999): 1 (online edition).

4. Burge, "The Greatest Story Never Read," 2.

5. Burge, "The Greatest Story Never Read," 6.

6. Michael S. Horton, "Recovering the Plumb Line," in John H. Armstrong, ed., *The Coming Evangelical Crisis* (Chicago: Moody, 1997), 253.

7. John Ortberg, *The Life You've Always Wanted* (Grand Rapids: Zondervan, 1997), 188.

8. R. Kent Hughes, "Preaching God's Word to the Church Today," in John H. Armstrong, ed., *The Coming Evangelical Crisis* (Chicago, Moody, 1997), 93.

9. Lutzer, *Seven Reasons,* 202.

10. Lutzer, *Seven Reasons,* 202.

11. *Chicago Tribune*, 23 July 2001.

12. F. F. Bruce, quoted in Josh McDowell, *Evidence That Demands a Verdict* (San Bernardino, Calif.: Campus Crusade for Christ, 1972), 19.

13. Bob Russell, *When God Builds a Church* (West Monroe, La.: Howard, 2000), 25.

14. R. Fowler White, "Does God Speak Today Apart from the Bible?" in John H. Armstrong, ed., *The Coming Evangelical Crisis* (Chicago, Moody, 1997), 87.

15. Howard G. Hendricks and William D. Hendricks, *Living by the Book* (Chicago: Moody, 1991), 9-10.

16. Gordon MacDonald, quoted in David Jeremiah, *Prayer: The Great Adventure* (Sisters, Oreg.: Multnomah, 1999), 226.

17. Gordon Gilkey, quoted in David Jeremiah, *Slaying the Giants in Your Life* (Nashville: Nelson, W Publishing Group, 2001), 159.

18. Madame Guyon, quoted in Ortberg, *The Life You've Always Wanted*, 182-3.

19. Charles R. Swindoll, *Elijah* (Nashville: Nelson, W Publishing Group, 2000), 94.

20. John Stott, quoted in Erwin W. Lutzer, *Ten Lies About God* (Nashville: Nelson, W Publishing Group, 2000), 80-1.

CHAPTER 6

1. Bill Hybels, "Why We Shouldn't Give Up on Prayer," *Preaching Today*, no. 184 (1998), audiotape.

2. Richard J. Foster, *Prayer* (San Francisco: HarperSanFrancisco, 1992), 7.

3. Brother Lawrence, quoted in John Ortberg, *The Life You've Always Wanted* (Grand Rapids: Zondervan, 1997), 96.

4. Greg Laurie, *The Upside-Down Church* (Wheaton, Ill.: Tyndale, 1999), 185-6.

5. William Evans, *Why Pray?* quoted in James Montgomery Boice, *Romans*, vol. 4 (Grand Rapids: Baker, 1995), 1898.

6. Lewis Smedes, quoted in Ortberg, *The Life You've Always Wanted,* 131.

7. This outline of the Lord's Prayer is not my original work. Authors including John MacArthur and David Jeremiah have used variations of it.

8. Foster, *Prayer,* 8.

9. Max Lucado, *Just Like Jesus* (Nashville: Nelson, W Publishing Group, 1998), 71.

10. Thomas Kelly, quoted in Gordon MacDonald, *Ordering Your Private World* (Nashville: Nelson, W Publishing Group, 1997)

CHAPTER 7

1. George Gallup Jr., "George Gallup Polls America on Religion," *Christianity Today* (1981): 6.

2. Dorothy Sayers, quoted in Philip Yancey, *Disappointment with God* (Grand Rapids: Zondervan, 1988), 147.

3. J. B. Phillips, quoted in Jim Cymbala, *Fresh Wind, Fresh Fire* (Grand Rapids: Zondervan, 1997), 73-4.

4. Donald McCullough, quoted in David Jeremiah, *Prayer: The Great Adventure* (Sisters, Oreg.: Multnomah, 1999), 90-1.

5. Bob Russell, *When God Builds a Church* (West Monroe, La.: Howard, 2000), 42.

6. Russell, *When God Builds a Church,* 43.

7. Russell, *When God Builds a Church,* 41.

8. Leith Anderson, quoted in David Jeremiah, *Slaying the Giants in Your Life* (Nashville: Nelson, W Publishing Group, 2001), 31.

9. Anne Ortlund, *Up with Worship* (Nashville: Broadman & Holman, 2001), 3.

10. William Hendricks, *Exit Interviews: Revealing Stories of Why People are Leaving the Church* (Chicago: Moody Press, 1993), quoted in Russell, *When God Builds a Church,* 47.

11. James Rutz, "Let's Wipe Out All the Laymen." An advertisement in *Christianity Today* (n.p.).

12. John Stott, quoted in John H. Armstrong, ed., *The Coming Evangelical Crisis* (Chicago: Moody Press, 1997), 182.

13. Ortlund, *Up with Worship*, 93.

14. David Jeremiah, *A Bend in the Road* (Nashville: Nelson, W Publishing Group, 2000), 97.

15. Dietrich Bonhoeffer, quoted in John F. MacArthur, *The Freedom and Power of Forgiveness* (Wheaton, Ill.: Crossway, 1998), 150-1.

16. Max Lucado, *In the Eye of the Storm* (Nashville: Nelson, W Publishing Group, 1991), 56-7.

CHAPTER 8

1. Lewis Smedes, quoted in David Jeremiah, *Slaying the Giants in Your Life* (Nashville: Nelson, W Publishing Group, 2000), 122.

2. Rubin Carter, quoted in Jeremiah, *Slaying the Giants in Your Life*, 117.

3. E. Stanley Jones, quoted in Steve Farrar, *Finishing Strong* (Sisters, Oreg.: Multnomah, 1995), 10.

4. Charles R. Swindoll, *Laugh Again* (Nashville: Nelson, W Publishing Group, 1995), 200.

5. Elisabeth Elliot, quoted in Charles R. Swindoll, *The Mystery of God's Will* (Nashville: Nelson, W Publishing Group, 1999), 10.

6. Napoleon Hill, quoted in A. L. Williams, *All You Can Do Is All You Can Do* (New York: Ballantine, 1988), 241.

7. Jonathan Edwards, quoted in Philip Yancey, *Reaching for the Invisible God* (Grand Rapids: Zondervan, 2000), 231-2.

CHAPTER 9

1. Steven J. Lawson, *Faith Under Fire* (Wheaton, Ill.: Crossway, 1995), 180-1.

2. William Gurnall, quoted in John Eldredge, *Wild at Heart* (Nashville: Nelson, 2001), 153.

3. Eldredge, *Wild at Heart,* 49.

4. Martyn Lloyd-Jones, quoted in Steve Farrar, *Finishing Strong* (Sisters, Oreg.: Multnomah, 1995), 62-3.

5. François Fénelon, quoted in John Ortberg, *The Life You've Always Wanted* (Grand Rapids: Zondervan, 1997), 168.

6. Clifford Williams, quoted in Ortberg, *The Life You've Always Wanted,* 172.

7. Brennan Manning, quoted in Chap Clark, *The Performance Illusion* (Colorado Springs: NavPress, 1993), 133.

8. C. S. Lewis, quoted in Richard J. Foster, *Prayer* (San Francisco: HarperSanFrancisco, 1992), 181-2.

9. Haddon N. Robinson, ed., *Biblical Sermons* (Grand Rapids: Baker, 1989), 17.

10. Erwin W. Lutzer, *The Serpent of Paradise* (Chicago: Moody, 1996), 44.

11. Elisabeth Elliot, quoted in James Montgomery Boice, *Romans,* vol. 3 (Grand Rapids: Baker, 1993), 1442.

CHAPTER 10

1. Gordon MacDonald, *The Life God Blesses* (Nashville: Nelson, 1994), 53.

2. The characteristics of spiritual experiences were adapted from *The Life God Blesses* by Gordon MacDonald, 56-9.

3. J. I. Packer, *Keep in Step with the Spirit* (Old Tappan, N.J.: Revell, 1984), 66.

To learn more about WaterBrook Press and view
our catalog of products, log on to our Web site:
www.waterbrookpress.com

WATERBROOK
PRESS